Light Bites

The Cookbook Library

Flame Tree has been creating **family-friendly**, **classic** and **beginner recipes** for our best-selling cookbooks for over ten years now. Our mission is to offer you a wide range of **expert-tested** dishes, while providing **straightforward** step-by-step photos and clear images of the final dish so that you can match it to your own results. Further information is available at **FlameTreeRecipes.com**

Publisher & Creative Director: Nick Wells
Senior Editor: Catherine Taylor
Designer: Mike Spender
Production and Digital Design: Chris Herbert
With thanks to: Gina Steer and Victoria Garrard

This is a **FLAME TREE** Book

FLAME TREE PUBLISHING
Crabtree Hall, Crabtree Lane
Fulham, London SW6 6TY
United Kingdom
www.flametreepublishing.com

First published 2007

ISBN: 978-1-84451-725-1

A copy of the CIP data for this book is available from the British Library.

Printed in Singapore

Light Bites

Quick and Easy, Proven Recipes

FLAME TREE
PUBLISHING

Contents

Contents

Main Meals   **198**

Soups   **154**

Sweet Treats

Hygiene in the Kitchen

It is well worth remembering that many foods can carry some form of bacteria. In most cases, the worst it will lead to is a bout of food poisoning or gastroenteritis, although for certain groups this can be more serious. The risk can be reduced or eliminated by good food hygiene and proper cooking.

Do not buy food that is past its sell-by date and do not consume any food that is past its use-by date. When buying food, use the eyes and nose. If the food looks tired, limp or a bad colour or it has a rank, acrid or simply bad smell, do not buy or eat it under any circumstances.

Regularly clean, defrost and clear out the refrigerator or freezer – it is worth checking the packaging to see exactly how long each product is safe to freeze.

Dish cloths and tea towels must be washed and changed regularly. Ideally use disposable cloths which should be replaced on a daily basis. More durable cloths should be left

to soak in bleach, then washed in the washing machine on a boil wash.

Always keep your hands, cooking utensils and food preparation surfaces clean and never allow pets to climb on to any work surfaces.

Buying

Avoid bulk buying where possible, especially fresh produce such as meat, poultry, fish, fruit and vegetables unless buying for the freezer. Fresh foods lose their nutritional value rapidly so buying a little at a time minimises loss of nutrients. It also eliminates a packed refrigerator which reduces the effectiveness of the refrigeration process.

When buying frozen foods, ensure that they are not heavily iced on the outside. Place in the freezer as soon as possible after purchase.

Preparation

Make sure that all work surfaces and utensils are clean and dry. Separate chopping boards should be used for raw and cooked meats, fish and vegetables. It is worth washing all fruits and vegetables regardless of whether they are going to be eaten raw or lightly cooked. Do not reheat food more than once.

All poultry must be thoroughly thawed before cooking. Leave the food in the refrigerator until it is completely thawed. Once defrosted, the chicken should be cooked as soon as possible. The only time food can be refrozen is when the food has been thoroughly thawed then cooked. Once the food has cooled then it can be frozen again for one month.

All poultry and game (except for duck) must be cooked

thoroughly. When cooked the juices will run clear. Other meats, like minced meat and pork should be cooked right the way through. Fish should turn opaque, be firm in texture and break easily into large flakes.

Storing, Refrigerating and Freezing

Meat, poultry, fish, seafood and dairy products should all be refrigerated. The temperature of the refrigerator should be between 1–5°C/34–41°F while the freezer temperature should not rise above -18°C/-0.4°F. When refrigerating cooked food, allow it to cool down completely before refrigerating. Hot food will raise the temperature of the refrigerator and possibly affect or spoil other food stored in it.

Food within the refrigerator and freezer should always be covered. Raw and cooked food should be stored in separate parts of the refrigerator. Cooked food should be kept on the top shelves of the refrigerator, while raw meat, poultry and fish should be placed on bottom shelves to avoid drips and cross-contamination.

High-Risk Foods

Certain foods may carry risks to people who are considered vulnerable such as the elderly, the ill, pregnant women, babies and those suffering from a recurring illness. It is advisable to avoid those foods which belong to a higher-risk category.

There is a slight chance that some eggs carry the bacteria salmonella. Cook the eggs until both the yolk and the white are firm to eliminate this risk. Sauces including Hollandaise, mayonnaise, mousses, soufflés and meringues all use raw or lightly cooked eggs, as do custard-based dishes, ice creams and sorbets. These are all considered high-risk foods to the vulnerable groups mentioned above. Certain meats and poultry also carry the potential risk of salmonella and so should be cooked thoroughly until the juices run clear and there is no pinkness left. Unpasteurised products such as milk, cheese (especially soft cheese), pâté, meat (both raw and cooked) all have the potential risk of listeria and should be avoided.

When buying seafood, buy from a reputable source. Fish should have bright clear eyes, shiny skin and bright pink or red gills. The fish should feel stiff to the touch, with a slight smell of sea air and iodine. The flesh of fish steaks and fillets should be translucent with no signs of discolouration. Avoid any molluscs that are open or do not close when tapped lightly. Univalves such as cockles or winkles should withdraw into their shells when lightly prodded. Squid and octopus should have firm flesh and a pleasant sea smell.

Care is required when freezing seafood. It is imperative to check whether the fish has been frozen before. If it has been, then it should not be frozen again under any circumstances.

Nutrition
The Role of Essential Nutrients

A healthy and well-balanced diet is the body's primary energy source. In children, it constitutes the building blocks for future health as well as providing lots of energy. In adults, it encourages self-healing and regeneration within the body. A well-balanced diet will provide the body with all the essential nutrients it needs. This can be achieved by eating a variety of foods, demonstrated in the pyramid below:

Fats

milk, yogurt
and cheese

Proteins

meat, fish, poultry, eggs,
nuts and pulses

*Fruits and
Vegetables*

Starchy Carbohydrates

cereals, potatoes, bread, rice and pasta

Fats

Fats fall into two categories: saturated and unsaturated fats. It is very important that a healthy balance is achieved within the diet. Fats are an essential part of the diet and a source of energy and provide essential fatty acids and fat soluble vitamins. The right balance of fats should boost the body's immunity to infection and keep muscles, nerves and arteries in good condition. Saturated fats are of animal origin and are hard when stored at room temperature. They can be found in dairy produce, meat, eggs, margarines and hard white cooking fat (lard) as well as in manufactured products such as pies, biscuits and cakes. A high intake of saturated fat over many years has been proven to increase heart disease and high blood cholesterol levels and often leads to weight gain. The aim of a healthy diet is to keep the fat content low in the foods that we eat. Lowering the amount of saturated fat that we consume is very important, but this does not mean that it is good to consume lots of other types of fat.

There are two kinds of unsaturated fats: poly-unsaturated fats and monounsaturated fats. Poly-unsaturated fats include the following oils: safflower oil, soybean oil, corn oil and sesame oil. Within the poly-unsaturated group are Omega oils. The Omega-3 oils are of significant interest because they have been found to be particularly beneficial to coronary health and can encourage brain growth and development. Omega-3 oils are derived from oily fish such as salmon, mackerel, herring, pilchards and sardines. It is recommended that we should eat these types of fish at least once a week. However, for those who do not eat fish or who are vegetarians, liver oil supplements are available in most supermarkets and health shops. It is suggested that these supplements should be taken on a daily basis. The most popular oils that are high in monounsaturates are olive oil, sunflower oil and peanut oil. The Mediterranean diet, which is based on a diet high in mono-unsaturated fats, is recommended for heart health. Also, monounsaturated fats are known to help reduce the levels of LDL (the bad) cholestrol.

Proteins

Composed of amino acids (proteins' building bricks), proteins perform a wide variety of essential functions for the body including supplying energy and building and repairing tissues. Good sources of proteins are eggs, milk, yogurt, cheese, meat, fish, poultry, eggs, nuts and pulses. (See the second level of the pyramid.) Some of these foods, however, contain saturated fats. To strike a nutritional balance eat generous amounts of vegetable protein foods such as soya, beans, lentils, peas and nuts.

Fruits and Vegetables

Not only are fruits and vegetables the most visually appealing foods, but they are extremely good for us, providing essential vitamins and minerals essential for growth, repair and protection in the human body. Fruits and vegetables are low in calories and

are responsible for regulating the body's metabolic processes and controlling the composition of its fluids and cells.

Minerals

CALCIUM Important for healthy bones and teeth, nerve transmission, muscle contraction, blood clotting and hormone function. Calcium promotes a healthy heart, improves skin, relieves aching muscles and bones, maintains the correct acid-alkaline balance and reduces menstrual cramps. Good sources are dairy products, small bones of small fish, nuts, pulses, fortified white flours, breads and green leafy vegetables.

CHROMIUM Part of the glucose tolerance factor, chromium balances blood sugar levels, helps to normalise hunger and reduce cravings, improves lifespan, helps protect DNA and is essential for heart function. Good sources are brewer's yeast, wholemeal bread, rye bread, oysters, potatoes, green peppers, butter and parsnips.

IODINE Important for the manufacture of thyroid hormones and for normal development. Good sources of iodine are seafood, seaweed, milk and dairy products.

IRON As a component of haemoglobin, iron carries oxygen around the body. It is vital for normal growth and development. Good sources are liver, corned beef, red meat, fortified breakfast cereals, pulses, green leafy vegetables, egg yolk and cocoa and cocoa products.

MAGNESIUM Important for efficient functioning of metabolic enzymes and development of the skeleton. Magnesium promotes healthy muscles by helping them to relax and is therefore good for PMS. It is also important for heart muscles and the nervous system. Good sources are nuts, green vegetables, meat, cereals, milk and yogurt.

PHOSPHORUS Forms and maintains bones and teeth, builds muscle tissue, helps maintain the body's pH and aids metabolism and energy production. Phosphorus is present in almost all foods.

POTASSIUM Enables nutrients to move into cells, while waste products move out; promotes healthy nerves and muscles; maintains fluid balance in the body; helps secretion of insulin for blood sugar control to produce constant energy; relaxes muscles; maintains heart functioning and stimulates gut movement to encourage proper elimination. Good sources are fruit, vegetables, milk and bread.

SELENIUM Antioxidant properties help to protect against free radicals and carcinogens. Selenium reduces inflammation, stimulates the immune system to fight infections, promotes a healthy heart and helps vitamin E's action. It is also required for the male reproductive system and is needed for metabolism. Good sources are tuna, liver, kidney, meat, eggs, cereals, nuts and dairy products.

SODIUM Important in helping to control body fluid and balance, preventing dehydration. Sodium is involved in muscle and nerve function and helps move nutrients into cells. All foods are good sources, however processed, pickled and salted foods are richest in sodium.

ZINC Important for metabolism and the healing of wounds. It also aids ability to cope with stress, promotes a healthy nervous system and brain especially in the growing foetus, aids bones and teeth formation and is essential for constant energy. Good sources are liver, meat, pulses, whole-grain cereals, nuts and oysters.

Vitamins

VITAMIN A Important for cell growth and development and for the formation of visual pigments in the eye. Vitamin A comes in two forms: retinol and beta-carotenes. Retinol is found in liver, meat and meat products and whole milk and its products. Beta-carotene is a powerful antioxidant and is found in red and yellow fruits and vegetables such as carrots, mangoes and apricots.

VITAMIN B1 Important in releasing energy from carboydrate-containing foods. Good sources are yeast and yeast products, bread, fortified breakfast cereals and potatoes.

VITAMIN B2 Important for metabolism of proteins, fats and carbohydrates to produce energy. Good sources are meat, yeast extracts, fortified breakfast cereals and milk and its products.

VITAMIN B3 Required for the metabolism of food into energy production. Good sources are milk and milk products, fortified breakfast cereals, pulses, meat, poultry and eggs.

VITAMIN B5 Important for the metabolism of food and energy production. All foods are good sources but especially fortified breakfast cereals, whole-grain bread and dairy products.

VITAMIN B6 Important for metabolism of protein and fat. Vitamin B6 may also be involved with the regulation of sex hormones. Good sources are liver, fish, pork, soya beans and peanuts.

VITAMIN B12 Important for the production of red blood cells and DNA. It is vital for growth and the nervous system. Good sources are meat, fish, eggs, poultry and milk.

BIOTIN Important for metabolism of fatty acids. Good sources of biotin are liver, kidney, eggs and nuts. Micro-organisms also manufacture this vitamin in the gut.

VITAMIN C Important for healing wounds and the formation of collagen which keeps skin and bones strong. It is an important antioxidant. Good sources are fruits, soft summer fruits and vegetables.

VITAMIN D Important for absorption and handling of calcium to help build bone strength. Good sources are oily fish, eggs, whole milk and milk products, margarine and of course sufficient exposure to sunlight, as vitamin D is made in the skin.

VITAMIN E Important as an antioxidant vitamin helping to protect cell membranes from damage. Good sources are vegetable oils, margarines, seeds, nuts and green vegetables.

FOLIC ACID Critical during pregnancy for the development of the brain and nerves. It is always essential for brain and nerve function and is needed for utilising protein and red blood cell formation. Good sources are whole-grain cereals, fortified breakfast cereals, green leafy vegetables, oranges and liver.

VITAMIN K Important for controlling blood clotting. Good sources are cauliflower, Brussels sprouts, lettuce, cabbage, beans, broccoli, peas, asparagus, potatoes, corn oil, tomatoes and milk.

Carbohydrates

Carbohydrates are an energy source and come in two forms: starch and sugar carbohydrates. Starch carbohydrates are also known as complex carbohydrates and they include all cereals, potatoes, breads, rice and pasta. (See the fourth level of the pyramid). Eating whole-grain varieties of these foods also provides fibre. Diets high in fibre are believed to be beneficial in helping to prevent bowel cancer and can also keep cholesterol down. High-fibre diets are also good for those concerned about weight gain. Fibre is bulky so fills the stomach, therefore reducing hunger pangs. Sugar carbohydrates, which are also known as fast-release carbohydrates (because of the quick fix of energy they give to the body), include sugar and sugar-sweetened products such as jams and syrups. Milk provides lactose, which is a milk sugar, and fruits provide fructose, which is a fruit sugar.

Finger Food

Moo Shi Pork

SERVES 4

175 g/6 oz pork fillet
2 tsp Chinese rice wine or
   dry sherry
2 tbsp light soy sauce
1 tsp cornflour
25 g/1 oz dried golden
   needles (day lily buds),
   soaked and drained

2 tbsp groundnut oil
3 medium eggs,
   lightly beaten
1 tsp freshly grated
   root ginger
3 spring onions, trimmed
   and thinly sliced
150 g/5 oz bamboo shoots,

cut into fine strips
salt and freshly ground
   black pepper
8 mandarin pancakes,
   steamed
hoisin sauce
sprigs of fresh coriander,
   to garnish

Cut the pork across the grain into 1 cm/½ inch slices, then cut into thin strips. Place in a bowl with the Chinese rice wine or sherry, soy sauce and cornflour. Mix well and reserve. Trim off the tough ends of the golden needles, then cut in half and reserve.

Heat a wok or large frying pan, add 1 tablespoon of the groundnut oil and, when hot, add the lightly beaten eggs, and cook for 1 minute, stirring all the time, until scrambled. Remove and reserve. Wipe the wok clean with absorbent kitchen paper.

Return the wok to the heat, add the remaining oil and when hot transfer the pork strips from the marinade mixture to the wok, shaking off as much marinade as possible. Stir-fry for 30 seconds, then add the ginger, spring onions, bamboo shoots and golden needles, and pour in the marinade. Stir-fry for 2–3 minutes or until cooked.

Return the scrambled eggs to the wok, season to taste with salt and pepper and stir for a few seconds until mixed well and heated through. Divide the mixture between the pancakes, drizzle each with 1 teaspoon of hoisin sauce and roll up. Garnish and serve immediately.

Try this: FOR AN ALTERNATIVE: 44   FOR A MORE SUBSTANTIAL OPTION: 204

Fried Pork–filled Wontons

MAKES 24

For the filling:
275 g/10 oz cooked pork,
　　finely chopped
2–3 spring onions, trimmed
　　and finely chopped
2.5 cm/1 inch piece fresh
　　root ginger, grated
1 garlic clove, peeled
　　and crushed
1 small egg, lightly beaten
1 tbsp soy sauce

1 tsp soft light brown sugar
1 tsp sweet chilli sauce or
　　tomato ketchup
24–30 wonton wrappers,
　　8 cm/3½ inches square
300 ml/½ pint vegetable oil
　　for deep frying

For the ginger dipping sauce:
4 tbsp soy sauce
1–2 tbsp rice or

　　raspberry vinegar
2.5 cm/1 inch piece fresh
　　root ginger, peeled and
　　finely slivered
1 tbsp sesame oil
1 tbsp soft light brown sugar
2–3 dashes hot chilli sauce
spring onion tassels,
　　to garnish

Place all the filling ingredients into a food processor and, using the pulse button, process until well blended. Do not overwork, the filling should have a coarse texture.

Lay out the wonton wrappers on a clean chopping board and put a teaspoon of the filling in the centre of each. Brush the edges with a little water and fold 2 opposite corners of each square over the filling to form a triangle, pressing the edges firmly to seal. Dampen the 2 other corners and overlap them slightly, pressing firmly to seal, to form an oven-envelope shape, similar to a tortellini.

For the dipping sauce, stir together all the ingredients until the sugar is dissolved. Pour into a serving bowl and reserve.

Heat the oil in a large wok to 190˚C/375˚F, or until a small cube of bread browns in about 30 seconds. Working in batches of 5–6, fry until the wontons are crisp and golden, turning once or twice. Remove and drain on absorbent kitchen paper. Garnish with spring onion tassels and serve hot with the dipping sauce.

 Try This: FOR AN ALTERNATIVE: 50　FOR A MORE SUBSTANTIAL OPTION: 202

Sticky Braised Spare Ribs

SERVES 4

900 g/2 lb meaty pork spare
　ribs, cut crossways into
　7.5 cm/3 inch pieces
125 ml/4 fl oz apricot or
　orange juice
50 ml/2 fl oz dry white wine
3 tbsp black bean sauce

3 tbsp tomato ketchup
2 tbsp clear honey
3–4 spring onions,
　trimmed and chopped
2 garlic cloves, peeled
　and crushed
grated zest of 1 small orange

salt and freshly ground
　black pepper

To garnish:
spring onion tassels
lemon wedges

Put the spare ribs in the wok and add enough cold water to cover. Bring to the boil over a medium-high heat, skimming any scum that rises to the surface. Cover and simmer for 30 minutes, then drain and rinse the ribs.

Rinse and dry the wok and return the ribs to it. In a bowl, blend the apricot nectar or orange juice with the white wine, black bean sauce, tomato ketchup and the honey until smooth.

Stir in the spring onions, garlic cloves and grated orange zest. Stir well until mixed thoroughly.

Pour the mixture over the spare ribs in the wok and stir gently until the ribs are lightly coated. Place over a moderate heat and bring to the boil.

Cover then simmer, stirring occasionally, for 1 hour, or until the ribs are tender and the sauce is thickened and sticky. (If the sauce reduces too quickly or begins to stick, add water 1 tablespoon at a time until the ribs are tender.) Adjust the seasoning to taste, then transfer the ribs to a serving plate and garnish with spring onion tassels and lemon wedges. Serve immediately.

Try This: FOR AN ALTERNATIVE: 32   FOR A MORE SUBSTANTIAL OPTION: 202

Swedish Cocktail Meatballs

SERVES 4–6

50 g/2 oz butter
1 onion, peeled and
    finely chopped
50 g/2 oz fresh white
    breadcrumbs
1 medium egg, beaten

125 ml/4 fl oz double cream
salt and freshly ground
    black pepper
350 g/12 oz fresh lean
    beef mince
125 g/4 oz fresh pork mince

3–4 tbsp freshly chopped dill
½ tsp ground allspice
1 tbsp vegetable oil
125 ml/4 fl oz beef stock
cranberry or cream cheese
    and chive sauce, to serve

Heat half the butter in a large wok, add the onion and cook, stirring frequently, for 4–6 minutes, or until softened and beginning to colour. Transfer to a bowl and leave to cool.

Wipe out the wok with absorbent kitchen paper. Add the breadcrumbs and beaten egg with 1–2 tablespoons of cream to the softened onion. Season to taste with salt and pepper and stir until well blended. Using your fingertips crumble the beef and pork mince into the bowl. Add half the dill, the allspice and, using your hands, mix together until well blended. With dampened hands, shape the mixture into 2.5 cm/1 inch balls.

Melt the remaining butter in the wok and add the vegetable oil, swirling it to coat the side of the wok. Working in batches, add about one quarter to one third of the meatballs in a single layer and cook for 5 minutes, swirling and turning until golden and cooked. Transfer to a plate and continue with the remaining meatballs, transferring them to the plate as they are cooked.

Pour off the fat in the wok. Add the beef stock and bring to the boil, then boil until reduced by half, stirring and scraping up any browned bits from the bottom. Add the remaining cream and continue to simmer until slightly thickened and reduced. Stir in the remaining dill and season if necessary. Add the meatballs and simmer for 2–3 minutes, or until heated right through. Serve with cocktail sticks, with the sauce in a separate bowl for dipping if preferred.

Try This: FOR AN ALTERNATIVE: 30   FOR A MORE SUBSTANTIAL OPTION: 200

Bacon, Mushroom & Cheese Puffs

SERVES 4

1 tbsp olive oil
225 g/8 oz field mushrooms,
 wiped and roughly chopped
225 g/8 oz rindless streaky
 bacon, roughly chopped
2 tbsp freshly

chopped parsley
salt and freshly ground
 black pepper
350 g/12 oz ready-rolled
 puff pastry sheets,
 thawed if frozen

25 g/1 oz Emmenthal
 cheese, grated
1 medium egg, beaten
salad leaves such as rocket
 or watercress, to garnish
tomatoes, to serve

Preheat the oven to 200°C/400°F/Gas Mark 6. Heat the olive oil in a large frying pan.

Add the mushrooms and bacon and fry for 6–8 minutes until golden in colour. Stir in the parsley, season to taste with salt and pepper and allow to cool.

Roll the sheet of pastry on a lightly floured surface until a 30.5 cm/12 inch square. Cut the pastry into 4 equal squares. Stir the grated Emmenthal cheese into the mushroom mixture. Spoon a quarter of the mixture on to one half of each square. Brush the edges of the square with a little of the beaten egg.

Fold over the pastry to form a triangular parcel. Seal the edges well and place on a lightly oiled baking sheet. Repeat until the squares are done.

Make shallow slashes in the top of the pastry with a knife. Brush the parcels with the remaining beaten egg and cook in the preheated oven for 20 minutes, or until puffy and golden brown.

Serve warm or cold, garnished with the salad leaves and served with tomatoes.

Try This: FOR AN ALTERNATIVE: 54   FOR A MORE SUBSTANTIAL OPTION: 116

Mixed Satay Sticks

SERVES 4

12 large raw prawns
350 g/12 oz beef rump steak
1 tbsp lemon juice
1 garlic clove, peeled
    and crushed
pinch of salt
2 tsp soft dark brown sugar
1 tsp ground cumin

1 tsp ground coriander
¼ tsp ground turmeric
1 tbsp groundnut oil
fresh coriander leaves,
    to garnish

For the spicy peanut sauce:
1 shallot, peeled and very

    finely chopped
1 tsp demerara sugar
50 g/2 oz creamed coconut,
    chopped
pinch of chilli powder
1 tbsp dark soy sauce
125 g/4 oz crunchy
    peanut butter

Preheat the grill on high just before required. Soak 8 bamboo skewers in cold water for at least 30 minutes. Peel the prawns, leaving the tails on. Using a sharp knife, remove the black vein along the back of the prawns. Cut the beef into 1 cm/½ inch wide strips. Place the prawns and beef in separate bowls and sprinkle each with ½ tablespoon of the lemon juice.

Mix together the garlic, pinch of salt, sugar, cumin, coriander, turmeric and groundnut oil to make a paste. Lightly brush over the prawns and beef. Cover and place in the refrigerator to marinate for at least 30 minutes, but for longer if possible.

Meanwhile, make the sauce. Pour 125 ml/4 fl oz of water into a small saucepan, add the shallot and sugar and heat gently until the sugar has dissolved. Stir in the creamed coconut and chilli powder. When melted, remove from the heat and stir in the soy sauce and the peanut butter. Leave to cool slightly, then spoon into a serving dish.

Thread 3 prawns on to each of 4 skewers and divide the sliced beef between the remaining skewers. Cook the skewers under the grill for 4–5 minutes, turning occasionally. The prawns should be opaque and pink and the beef browned on the outside, but still pink in the centre. Transfer to warmed serving plates, garnish with fresh coriander and serve immediately with the warm sauce.

Try This: FOR AN ALTERNATIVE: 58   FOR A MORE SUBSTANTIAL OPTION: 286

Coriander Chicken & Soy Sauce Cakes

SERVES 4

¼ cucumber, peeled
1 shallot, peeled and
   thinly sliced
6 radishes, trimmed
   and sliced
350 g/12 oz skinless
   boneless chicken thigh

4 tbsp roughly chopped
   fresh coriander
2 spring onions, trimmed
   and roughly chopped
1 red chilli, deseeded
   and chopped
finely grated rind of ½ lime

2 tbsp soy sauce
1 tbsp caster sugar
2 tbsp rice vinegar
1 red chilli, deseeded and
   finely sliced
freshly chopped coriander,
   to garnish

Preheat the oven to 190°C/375°F/Gas Mark 5. Halve the cucumber lengthwise, deseed and dice.

In a bowl mix the shallot and radishes. Chill until ready to serve with the diced cucumber.

Place the chicken thighs in a food processor and blend until coarsely chopped. Add the coriander and spring onions to the chicken with the chilli, lime rind and soy sauce. Blend again until mixed.

Using slightly damp hands, shape the chicken mixture into 12 small rounds. Place the rounds on a lightly oiled baking tray and bake in the preheated oven for 15 minutes, until golden.

In a small pan heat the sugar with 2 tablespoons of water until dissolved. Simmer until syrupy. Remove from the heat and allow to cool a little, then stir in the vinegar and chilli slices. Pour over the cucumber and the radish and shallot salad. Garnish with the chopped coriander and serve the chicken cakes with the salad immediately.

Try This: FOR AN ALTERNATIVE: 24   FOR A MORE SUBSTANTIAL OPTION: 214

Deep–fried Chicken Wings

SERVES 4

2 tsp turmeric
1 tsp hot chilli powder
1 tsp ground coriander
1 tsp ground cumin
3 garlic cloves,
    peeled and crushed

8 chicken wings
2 tbsp orange marmalade
2 tbsp ginger preserve
   or marmalade
1 tsp salt
3 tbsp rice wine vinegar

2 tbsp tomato ketchup
1 litre/1¾ pints vegetable oil
   for deep frying
lime wedges, to garnish

Blend the turmeric, chilli powder, ground coriander, ground cumin and garlic together in a small bowl. Dry the chicken wings thoroughly, using absorbent kitchen paper, then rub the spice mixture onto the skin of each chicken wing. Cover and chill in the refrigerator for at least 2 hours.

Meanwhile make the dipping sauce by mixing together the marmalade, ginger preserve, salt, rice wine vinegar and tomato ketchup in a small saucepan. Heat until blended, leave to cool, then serve. If using straightaway, spoon into a small dipping bowl, but if using later pour into a container with a close-fitting lid and store in the refrigerator.

Pour the oil into the wok and heat to 190˚C/375˚F, or until a small cube of bread dropped in the oil turns golden brown in 30 seconds. Cook 2–3 chicken wings at a time, lowering them into the hot oil, and frying for 3–4 minutes. Remove the wings, using a slotted spoon, and drain on absorbent kitchen paper. You may need to reheat the oil before cooking each batch.

When all the chicken wings are cooked, arrange on a warmed serving dish, garnish with the lime wedges and serve.

Try This: FOR AN ALTERNATIVE: 40   FOR A MORE SUBSTANTIAL OPTION: 216

Hoisin Chicken Pancakes

SERVES 4

3 tbsp hoisin sauce
1 garlic clove, peeled
   and crushed
2.5 cm/1 inch piece root
   ginger, peeled and
   finely grated
1 tbsp soy sauce

1 tsp sesame oil
salt and freshly ground
   black pepper
4 skinless chicken thighs
½ cucumber, peeled
   (optional)
12 bought Chinese pancakes

6 spring onions, trimmed
   and cut lengthways into
   fine shreds
sweet chilli dipping sauce,
   to serve

Preheat the oven to 190°C/375°F/Gas Mark 5. In a non-metallic bowl, mix the hoisin sauce with the garlic, ginger, soy sauce, sesame oil and seasoning.

Add the chicken thighs and turn to coat in the mixture. Cover loosely and leave in the refrigerator to marinate for 3–4 hours, turning the chicken from time to time.

Remove the chicken from the marinade and place in a roasting tin. Reserve the marinade. Bake in the preheated oven for 30 minutes basting occasionally with the marinade.

Cut the cucumber in half lengthways and remove the seeds by running a teaspoon down the middle to scoop them out. Cut into thin batons.

Place the pancakes in a steamer to warm or heat according to packet instructions. Thinly slice the hot chicken and arrange on a plate with the shredded spring onions, cucumber and pancakes.

Place a spoonful of the chicken in the middle of each warmed pancake and top with pieces of cucumber, spring onion, and a little dipping sauce. Roll up and serve immediately.

Try This: FOR AN ALTERNATIVE: 68   FOR A MORE SUBSTANTIAL OPTION: 88

Crostini with Chicken Livers

SERVES 4

2 tbsp olive oil
2 tbsp butter
1 shallot, peeled and
    finely chopped
1 garlic clove,
    peeled and crushed
150 g/5 oz chicken livers
1 tbsp plain flour

2 tbsp dry white wine
1 tbsp brandy
50 g/2 oz mushrooms, sliced
salt and freshly ground
    black pepper
4 slices of ciabatta
    or similar bread

To garnish:
fresh sage leaves
lemon wedges

Heat 1 tablespoon of the olive oil and 1 tablespoon of the butter in a frying pan, add the shallot and garlic and cook gently for 2–3 minutes.

Trim and wash the chicken livers thoroughly and pat dry on absorbent kitchen paper as much as possible. Cut into slices, then toss in the flour. Add the livers to the frying pan with the shallot and garlic and continue to fry for a further 2 minutes, stirring continuously.

Pour in the white wine and brandy and bring to the boil. Boil rapidly for 1–2 minutes to allow the alcohol to evaporate, then stir in the sliced mushrooms and cook gently for about 5 minutes, or until the chicken livers are cooked, but just a little pink inside. Season to taste with salt and pepper.

Fry the slices of ciabatta or similar-style bread in the remaining oil and butter, then place on individual serving dishes. Spoon over the liver mixture and garnish with a few sage leaves and lemon wedges. Serve immediately.

Try This: FOR AN ALTERNATIVE: 78   FOR A MORE SUBSTANTIAL OPTION: 146

Shredded Duck in Lettuce Leaves

SERVES 4–6

15 g/½ oz dried Chinese (shiitake) mushrooms
2 tbsp vegetable oil
400 g/14 oz boneless, skinless duck breast, cut crossways into thin strips
1 red chilli, deseeded and thinly sliced diagonally

4–6 spring onions, trimmed and diagonally sliced
2 garlic cloves, peeled and crushed
75 g/3 oz beansprouts
3 tbsp soy sauce
1 tbsp Chinese rice wine or dry sherry

1–2 tsp clear honey or brown sugar
4–6 tbsp hoisin sauce
large, crisp lettuce leaves such as iceberg or cos
handful of fresh mint leaves
dipping sauce (*see* Sesame Prawns, page 44)

Cover the dried Chinese mushrooms with almost boiling water, leave for 20 minutes, then drain and slice thinly.

Heat a large wok, add the oil and when hot stir-fry the duck for 3–4 minutes, or until sealed. Remove with a slotted spoon and reserve.

Add the chilli, spring onions, garlic and Chinese mushrooms to the wok and stir-fry for 2–3 minutes, or until softened. Add the beansprouts, the soy sauce, Chinese rice wine or dry sherry and honey or brown sugar to the wok, and continue to stir-fry for 1 minute, or until blended.

Stir in the reserved duck and stir-fry for 2 minutes, or until well mixed together and heated right through. Transfer to a heated serving dish.

Arrange the hoisin sauce in a small bowl on a tray or plate with a pile of lettuce leaves and the mint leaves. Let each guest spoon a little hoisin sauce onto a lettuce leaf, then top with a large spoonful of the stir-fried duck and vegetables and roll up the leaf to enclose the filling. Serve with the dipping sauce.

Try This: FOR AN ALTERNATIVE: 70   FOR A MORE SUBSTANTIAL OPTION: 220

Tempura

SERVES 4

For the batter:
200 g/7 oz plain flour
pinch of bicarbonate of soda
1 medium egg yolk

For the prawns & vegetables:
8–12 raw king size prawns

1 carrot, peeled
125 g/4 oz button
   mushrooms, wiped
1 green pepper, deseeded
1 small aubergine, trimmed
1 onion, peeled
125 g/4 oz French beans

125 ml/4 fl oz sesame oil
300 ml/½ pint vegetable oil
   for deep frying

To serve:
soy sauce
chilli dipping sauce

Sift the flour and bicarbonate of soda into a mixing bowl. Blend 450 ml/¾ pint water and the egg yolk together, then gradually whisk into the flour mixture until a smooth batter is formed.

Peel the prawns, leaving the tails intact, de-vein, then rinse lightly and pat dry with absorbent kitchen paper and reserve. Slice the carrot thinly then, using small pastry cutters, cut out fancy shapes. Cut the mushrooms in half, if large, and cut the pepper into chunks. Slice the aubergine, then cut into chunks, together with the onion, and finally trim the French beans.

Pour the sesame oil and the vegetable oil into a large wok and heat to 180°C/350°F, or until a small spoonful of the batter dropped into the oil sizzles and cooks on impact.

Dip the prawns and vegetables into the reserved batter (no more than 8 pieces at a time) and stir until lightly coated. Cook for 3 minutes, turning occasionally during cooking, or until evenly golden. Using a slotted spoon, transfer the prawns and vegetables onto absorbent kitchen paper and drain well. Keep warm. Repeat with the remaining ingredients. Serve immediately with soy sauce and chilli dipping sauce.

Try This: FOR AN ALTERNATIVE: 44   FOR A MORE SUBSTANTIAL OPTION: 102

Sweet-&-Sour Battered Fish

SERVES 4–6

450 g/1 lb cod fillet, skinned
150 g/5 oz plain flour
salt and freshly ground
   black pepper
2 tbsp cornflour
2 tbsp arrowroot

vegetable oil for deep-frying

For the sweet-&-sour sauce:
4 tbsp orange juice
2 tbsp white wine vinegar
2 tbsp dry sherry

1 tbsp dark soy sauce
1 tbsp soft light brown sugar
2 tsp tomato purée
1 red pepper, deseeded
   and diced
2 tsp cornflour

Cut the fish into pieces about 5 cm x 2.5 cm/2 x 1 inch. Place 4 tablespoons of the flour in a small bowl, season with salt and pepper to taste, then add the fish strips a few at a time and toss until coated.

Sift the remaining flour into a bowl with a pinch of salt, the cornflour and arrowroot. Gradually whisk in 300 ml/½ pint iced water to make a smooth, thin batter.

Heat the oil in a wok or deep-fat fryer to 190°C/375°F. Working in batches, dip the fish strips in the batter and deep-fry them for 3–5 minutes, or until crisp. Using a slotted spoon, remove the strips and drain on absorbent kitchen paper.

Meanwhile, make the sauce. Place 3 tablespoons of the orange juice, the vinegar, sherry, soy sauce, sugar, tomato purée and red pepper in a small saucepan. Bring to the boil, lower the heat and simmer for 3 minutes.

Blend the cornflour with the remaining orange juice, stir into the sauce and simmer, stirring, for 1 minute or until thickened. Arrange the fish on a warmed platter or individual plates. Drizzle a little of the sauce over and serve immediately with the remaining sauce.

Sesame Prawns

SERVES 6–8

24 large raw prawns
40 g/1 oz plain flour
4 tbsp sesame seeds
salt and freshly ground
   black pepper
1 large egg

300 ml/½ pint vegetable oil
   for deep frying

For the soy dipping sauce:
50 ml/2 fl oz soy sauce
1 spring onion, trimmed

   and finely chopped
½ tsp dried crushed chillies
1 tbsp sesame oil
1–2 tsp sugar, or to taste
strips of spring onion,
   to garnish

Remove the heads from the prawns by twisting away from the body and discard. Peel the prawns, leaving the tails on for presentation. Using a sharp knife, remove the black vein from the back of the prawns. Rinse and dry. Slice along the back, but do not cut through the prawn body. Place on the chopping board and press firmly to flatten slightly and make a butterfly shape.

Put the flour, half the sesame seeds, salt and pepper into a food processor and blend for 30 seconds. Tip into a polythene bag and add the prawns, 4–5 at a time. Twist to seal, then shake to coat with the flour.

Beat the egg in a small bowl with the remaining sesame seeds, salt and pepper.

Heat the oil in a large wok to 190°C/ 375°F, or until a small cube of bread browns in about 30 seconds. Working in batches of 5 or 6, and holding each prawn by the tail, dip into the beaten egg, then carefully lower into the oil. Cook for 1–2 minutes, or until crisp and golden, turning once or twice. Using a slotted spoon, remove the prawns, drain on absorbent kitchen paper and keep warm.

To make the dipping sauce, stir together the soy sauce, spring onion, chillies, oil and sugar until the sugar dissolves. Arrange the prawns on a plate, garnish with strips of spring onion and serve immediately.

Try This: FOR AN ALTERNATIVE: 40   FOR A MORE SUBSTANTIAL OPTION: 102

Prawn Toasts

SERVES 8–10

225 g/8 oz cooked peeled
  prawns, thawed if frozen,
  well drained and dried
1 medium egg white
2 spring onions, trimmed
  and chopped
1 cm/½ inch piece fresh root
  ginger, peeled and chopped

1 garlic clove, peeled
  and chopped
1 tsp cornflour
2–3 dashes hot pepper sauce
½ tsp sugar
salt and freshly ground
  black pepper
8 slices firm-textured

white bread
4–5 tbsp sesame seeds
300 ml/½ pint vegetable oil
  for deep frying
sprigs of fresh coriander,
  to garnish

Put the prawns, egg white, spring onions, ginger, garlic, cornflour, hot pepper sauce and sugar into a food processor. Season to taste with about ½ teaspoon of salt and black pepper. Process until the mixture forms a smooth paste, scraping down the side of the bowl once or twice.

Using a metal palette knife, spread an even layer of the paste over the bread slices. Sprinkle each slice generously with sesame seeds, pressing gently to bury them in the paste.

Trim the crusts off each slice, then cut each slice diagonally into 4 triangles. Cut each triangle in half again to make 8 pieces from each slice.

Heat the vegetable oil in a large wok to 190°C/375°F, or until a small cube of bread browns in about 30 seconds. Working in batches, fry the prawn triangles for 30–60 seconds, or until they are golden, turning once.

Remove with a slotted spoon and drain on absorbent kitchen paper. Keep the toasts warm. Arrange them on a large serving plate and garnish with sprigs of fresh coriander. Serve immediately.

Try This: FOR AN ALTERNATIVE: 44   FOR A MORE SUBSTANTIAL OPTION: 172

Quick Mediterranean Prawns

SERVES 4

20 raw Mediterranean prawns
3 tbsp olive oil
1 garlic clove, peeled and
   crushed
finely grated zest and
   juice of ½ lemon
sprigs of fresh rosemary

**For the pesto & sun-dried
   tomato dips:**
150 ml/¼ pint Greek
   style yogurt
1 tbsp prepared pesto
150 ml/¼ pint crème fraîche
1 tbsp sun-dried

tomato paste
1 tbsp wholegrain mustard
salt and freshly ground
   black pepper
lemon wedges,
   to garnish

Remove the shells from the prawns, leaving the tail shells. Using a small, sharp knife, remove the dark vein that runs along the back of the prawns. Rinse and drain on absorbent kitchen paper.

Whisk 2 tablespoons of the oil with the garlic, lemon zest and juice in a small bowl. Bruise 1 sprig of rosemary with a rolling pin and add to the bowl. Add the prawns, toss to coat, then cover and leave to marinate in the refrigerator until needed.

For the simple dips, mix the yogurt and pesto in one bowl and the crème fraîche, tomato paste and mustard in another bowl. Season to taste with salt and pepper.

Heat a wok, add the remaining oil and swirl round to coat the sides. Remove the prawns from the marinade, leaving any juices and the rosemary behind. Add to the wok and stir-fry over a high heat for 3–4 minutes, or until the prawns are pink and just cooked through.

Remove the prawns from the wok and arrange on a platter. Garnish with lemon wedges and more fresh rosemary sprigs and serve hot or cold with the dips.

Try This: FOR AN ALTERNATIVE: 44   FOR A MORE SUBSTANTIAL OPTION: 104

Deep–fried Crab Wontons

MAKES 24–30

2 tbsp sesame oil
6–8 water chestnuts, rinsed,
  drained and chopped
2 spring onions, peeled and
  finely chopped
1 cm/½ inch piece fresh root
  ginger, peeled and grated
185 g can white

crabmeat, drained
50 ml/2 fl oz soy sauce
2 tbsp rice wine vinegar
½ tsp dried crushed chillies
2 tsp sugar
½ tsp hot pepper sauce,
  or to taste
1 tbsp freshly chopped

coriander or dill
1 large egg yolk
1 packet wonton skins
vegetable oil for deep-frying
lime wedges, to garnish
dipping sauce, to serve

Heat a wok or large frying pan, add 1 tablespoon of the sesame oil and, when hot, add the water chestnuts, spring onions and ginger and stir-fry for 1 minute. Remove from the heat and leave to cool slightly.

In a bowl, mix the crabmeat with the soy sauce, vinegar, crushed chillies, sugar, hot pepper sauce, chopped coriander or dill and the egg yolk. Stir in the cooled stir-fried mixture until well blended.

Lay the wonton skins on a work surface and place 1 teaspoonful of the crab mixture in the centre of each. Brush the edges of each wonton skin with a little water and fold 1 corner to the opposite corner to form a triangle. Press to seal. Bring the 2 corners of the triangle together to meet in the centre, brush 1 with a little water and overlap them, pressing to seal and form a 'tortellini' shape. Place on a baking sheet and continue with the remaining triangles.

Pour enough oil into a large wok to come 5 cm/2 inches up the sides and place over a high heat. Working in batches of 5 or 6, fry the wontons for 3 minutes, or until crisp and golden, turning once or twice. Carefully remove the wontons with a slotted spoon, drain on absorbent kitchen paper and keep warm. Place on individual warmed serving plates, garnish each dish with a lime wedge and serve immediately with the dipping sauce.

Try This: FOR AN ALTERNATIVE: 20 FOR A MORE SUBSTANTIAL OPTION: 108

Thai Crab Cakes

SERVES 4

225 g/8 oz white and brown crabmeat (about equivalent to the flesh of 2 medium crabs)
1 tsp ground coriander
¼ tsp chilli powder
¼ tsp ground turmeric
2 tsp lime juice

1 tsp soft light brown sugar
2.5 cm/1 inch piece fresh root ginger, peeled and grated
3 tbsp freshly chopped coriander
2 tsp finely chopped lemon grass

2 tbsp plain flour
2 medium eggs, separated
50 g/2 oz fresh white breadcrumbs
3 tbsp groundnut oil
lime wedges, to garnish
mixed salad leaves, to serve

Place the crabmeat in a bowl with the ground coriander, chilli, turmeric, lime juice, sugar, ginger, chopped coriander, lemon grass, flour and egg yolks. Mix together well.

Divide the mixture into 12 equal portions and form each into a small patty about 5 cm/2 inches across. Lightly whisk the egg whites and put into a dish. Place the breadcrumbs on a separate plate.

Dip each crab cake, first in the egg whites, then in the breadcrumbs, turning to coat both sides. Place on a plate, cover and chill in the refrigerator until ready to cook.

Heat the oil in a large frying pan. Add 6 crab cakes and cook for 3 minutes on each side, or until crisp and golden brown on the outside and cooked through. Remove, drain on absorbent kitchen paper and keep warm while cooking the remaining cakes. Arrange on plates, garnish with lime wedges and serve immediately with salad leaves.

Try This: FOR AN ALTERNATIVE: 66   FOR A MORE SUBSTANTIAL OPTION: 166

Smoked Mackerel Vol–au–Vents

SERVES 1–2

350 g/12 oz prepared
   puff pastry
1 small egg, beaten
2 tsp sesame seeds
225 g/8 oz peppered smoked

mackerel, skinned
   and chopped
5 cm/2 inch piece cucumber
4 tbsp soft cream cheese
2 tbsp cranberry sauce

1 tbsp freshly chopped dill
1 tbsp finely grated
   lemon rind
dill sprigs, to garnish
mixed salad leaves, to serve

Preheat the oven to 230°C/450°F/Gas Mark 8. Roll the pastry out on a lightly floured surface and using a 9 cm/3½ inch fluted cutter, cut out 12 rounds.

Using a 1 cm/½ inch cutter mark a lid in the centre of each round.

Place on a damp baking sheet and brush the rounds with a little beaten egg.

Sprinkle the pastry with the sesame seeds and bake in the preheated oven for 10–12 minutes, or until golden brown and well risen.

Transfer the vol-au-vents to a chopping board and when cool enough to touch carefully remove the lids with a small sharp knife. Scoop out any uncooked pastry from the inside of each vol-au-vent, then return to the oven for 5–8 minutes to dry out. Remove and allow to cool.

Flake the mackerel into small pieces and reserve. Peel the cucumber if desired, cut into very small dice and add to the mackerel.

Beat the soft cream cheese with the cranberry sauce, dill and lemon rind. Stir in the mackerel and cucumber and use to fill the vol-au-vents. Place the lids on top and garnish dill sprigs.

 Try This: FOR AN ALTERNATIVE: 56   FOR A MORE SUBSTANTIAL OPTION: 242

Smoked Salmon Sushi

SERVES 4

125 g/4 oz sushi rice or
    round pudding rice
2 tbsp cider vinegar
1 tbsp caster sugar

1 tsp salt
2 green leeks, trimmed
225 g/8 oz smoked salmon
1 tsp Japanese soy sauce

To garnish:
fresh chives
lemon or lime wedges

Wash the rice in plenty of cold water, then drain. Put the rice and 200 ml/7 fl oz cold water in a saucepan and leave to soak for 30 minutes. Place the saucepan over a medium heat and bring to the boil, stirring frequently. Lower the heat, cover and cook the rice for about 15 minutes, or until the grains are tender and the water has been absorbed. Remove from the heat and leave, still covered, for a further 10–15 minutes.

Place the vinegar, sugar and salt in a small saucepan. Heat gently, stirring to dissolve the sugar. Turn the rice into a large bowl, sprinkle over the vinegar mixture and mix through the rice.

Cut the trimmed leeks in half lengthways, then blanch in boiling water for 3–4 minutes. Drain and place in ice-cold water for 5 minutes, then drain again.

Separate the leek leaves. Cut both the leek leaves and the salmon slices lengthways into 2.5 x 7.5 cm (1 x 3 inch) strips, reserving 2 wide leek leaves. Place the leek slices neatly on top of the sliced salmon.

Spoon the rice onto the salmon and leek slices, then roll into parcels. Using the tip of a sharp knife, slice the reserved leek leaves lengthways into long strips. Tie the strips around the smoked salmon parcels. Sprinkle the parcels with a few drops of the soy sauce, garnish with the chives and lemon wedges and serve.

Try This: FOR AN ALTERNATIVE: 54   FOR A MORE SUBSTANTIAL OPTION: 230

Citrus Monkfish Kebabs

SERVES 4

For the marinade:
1 tbsp sunflower oil
finely grated rind and juice
   of 1 lime
1 tbsp lemon juice
1 sprig of freshly
   chopped rosemary

1 tbsp whole-grain mustard
1 garlic clove, peeled
   and crushed
salt and freshly ground
   black pepper

For the kebabs:
450 g/1 lb monkfish tail
8 raw tiger prawns
1 small green courgette,
   trimmed and sliced
4 tbsp of half-fat crème
   fraîche

Preheat the grill and line the grill rack with tinfoil. Mix all the marinade ingredients together in a small bowl and reserve.

Using a sharp knife, cut down both sides of the monkfish tail. Remove the bone and discard. Cut away and discard any skin, then cut the monkfish into bite-sized cubes. Peel the prawns, leaving the tails intact and remove the thin black vein that runs down the back of each prawn. Place the fish and prawns in a shallow dish.

Pour the marinade over the fish and prawns. Cover lightly and leave to marinate in the refrigerator for 30 minutes. Spoon the marinade over the fish and prawns occasionally during this time. Soak the skewers in cold water for 30 minutes, then drain.

Thread the cubes of fish, prawns and courgettes on to the drained skewers. Arrange on the grill rack then place under the preheated grill and cook for 5–7 minutes, or until cooked thoroughly and the prawns have turned pink. Occasionally brush with the remaining marinade and turn the kebabs during cooking.

Mix 2 tablespoons of the marinade with the crème fraîche and serve as a dip with the kebabs.

Try This: FOR AN ALTERNATIVE: 28   FOR A MORE SUBSTANTIAL OPTION: 238

Wok–fried Snacks – Popcorn & Sesame–coated Pecans

SERVES 4–6

For the popcorn:
75 ml/ 3 fl oz vegetable oil
75 g/3 oz unpopped popcorn
½ tsp garlic salt
1 tsp hot chilli powder

For the pecans:
50 g/2 oz sugar
½ tsp ground cinnamon
½ tsp ground Chinese five
    spice powder

¼ tsp salt
¼ tsp cayenne pepper
175 g/6 oz pecan or
    walnut halves
sesame seeds for sprinkling

For the popcorn, heat half the oil in a large wok over a medium-high heat. Add 2–3 kernels and cover with a lid. When these kernels pop, add all the popcorn and cover tightly. Cook until the popping stops, shaking from time to time.

When the popping stops, pour the popped corn into a bowl and immediately add the remaining oil to the wok with the garlic salt and chilli powder. Stir-fry for 30 seconds, or until blended and fragrant.

Return the popcorn to the wok, stir-fry and toss for a further 30 seconds, or until coated. Pour into the bowl and serve warm or at room temperature.

For the pecans, put the sugar, cinnamon, Chinese five spice powder, salt and cayenne pepper into a large wok and stir in 50 ml/2 fl oz water. Bring to the boil over a high heat, then simmer for 4 minutes, stirring frequently.

Remove from the heat and stir in the pecans or walnuts until well coated. Turn onto a lightly oiled, non-stick baking sheet and sprinkle generously with the sesame seeds.

Working quickly with 2 forks, separate the nuts into individual pieces or bite-sized clusters. Sprinkle with a few more sesame seeds and leave to cool completely. Carefully remove from the baking sheet, breaking into smaller pieces if necessary.

Try This: FOR AN ALTERNATIVE: 62   FOR A MORE SUBSTANTIAL OPTION: 142

Mixed Canapés

SERVES 12

**For the stir-fried
cheese canapés:**
6 thick slices white bread
40 g/1½ oz butter, softened
75 g/3 oz mature Cheddar
   cheese, grated
75 g/3 oz blue cheese such

as Stilton or Gorgonzola,
   crumbled
3 tbsp sunflower oil

For the spicy nuts:
25 g/1 oz unsalted butter
2 tbsp light olive oil

450 g/1 lb mixed
   unsalted nuts
1 tsp ground paprika
½ tsp ground cumin
½ tsp fine sea salt
sprigs of fresh coriander,
   to garnish

For the cheese canapés, cut the crusts off the bread, then gently roll with a rolling pin to flatten slightly. Thinly spread with butter, then sprinkle over the mixed cheeses as evenly as possible.

Roll up each slice tightly, then cut into 4 slices, each about 2.5 cm/1 inch long. Heat the oil in a wok or large frying pan and stir-fry the cheese rolls in 2 batches, turning them all the time until golden brown and crisp. Drain on absorbent kitchen paper and serve warm or cold.

For the spicy nuts, melt the butter and oil in a wok, then add the nuts and stir-fry over a low heat for about 5 minutes, stirring all the time, or until they begin to colour.

Sprinkle the paprika and cumin over the nuts and continue stir-frying for a further 1–2 minutes, or until the nuts are golden brown.

Remove from the wok and drain on absorbent kitchen paper. Sprinkle with the salt, garnish with sprigs of fresh coriander and serve hot or cold. If serving cold, store both the cheese canapés and the spicy nuts in airtight containers.

Try This: FOR AN ALTERNATIVE: 60   FOR A MORE SUBSTANTIAL OPTION: 270

Corn Fritters with Hot & Spicy Relish

MAKES 16–20

325 g can sweetcorn
   kernels, drained
1 onion, peeled and very
   finely chopped
1 spring onion, trimmed and
   very finely chopped
½ tsp chilli powder
1 tsp ground coriander

4 tbsp plain flour
1 tsp baking powder
1 medium egg
salt and freshly ground
   black pepper
300 ml/½ pint groundnut oil
sprigs of fresh coriander,
   to garnish

For the spicy relish:
3 tbsp sunflower oil
1 onion, peeled and very
   finely chopped
¼ tsp dried crushed chillies
2 garlic cloves, peeled
   and crushed
2 tbsp plum sauce

First make the relish. Heat a wok, add the sunflower oil and when hot, add the onion and stir-fry for 3–4 minutes or until softened. Add the chillies and garlic, stir-fry for 1 minute, then leave to cool slightly. Stir in the plum sauce, transfer to a food processor and blend until the consistency of chutney. Reserve.

Place the sweetcorn into a food processor and blend briefly until just mashed. Transfer to a bowl with the onions, chilli powder, coriander, flour, baking powder and egg. Season to taste with salt and pepper and mix together.

Heat a wok, add the oil and heat to 180°C/350°F. Working in batches, drop a few spoonfuls of the sweetcorn mixture into the oil and deep-fry for 3–4 minutes, or until golden and crispy, turning occasionally. Using a slotted spoon, remove and drain on absorbent kitchen paper. Arrange on a warmed serving platter, garnish with sprigs of coriander and serve immediately with the relish.

Try This: FOR AN ALTERNATIVE: 66   FOR A MORE SUBSTANTIAL OPTION: 254

Thai Rice Cakes with Mango Salsa

SERVES 4

225 g/8 oz Thai fragrant rice
400 g can coconut milk
1 lemon grass stalk, bruised
2 kaffir lime leaves,
  shredded
1 tbsp vegetable oil, plus
  extra for deep frying
1 garlic clove, peeled and
  finely chopped

1 tsp freshly grated
  root ginger
1 red pepper, deseeded
  and finely chopped
2 red chillies, deseeded
  and finely chopped
1 medium egg, beaten
25 g/1 oz dried
  breadcrumbs

For the mango salsa:
1 large mango, peeled,
  stoned and finely chopped
1 small red onion, peeled
  and finely chopped
2 tbsp freshly
  chopped coriander
2 tbsp freshly chopped basil
juice of 1 lime

Wash the rice in several changes of water until the water stays relatively clear. Drain, place in a saucepan with a tight-fitting lid and add the coconut milk, lemon grass and lime leaves. Bring to the boil, cover and cook over the lowest possible heat for 10 minutes. Turn off the heat and leave to stand for 10 minutes, without lifting the lid.

Heat the wok, then add 1 tablespoon of oil and when hot, add the garlic, ginger, red pepper and half the chilli. Stir-fry for 1–2 minutes, until just softened, then place in a large bowl. When the rice is cooked, turn into the mixing bowl and add the egg. Season to taste with salt and pepper and mix together well. Put the breadcrumbs into a shallow dish. Form the rice mixture into 8 cakes and coat them in the breadcrumbs. Chill the cakes in the refrigerator for 30 minutes.

Meanwhile, make the mango salsa. In a bowl, mix together the mango, red onion, coriander, basil, lime juice and remaining red chilli and reserve.

Fill a clean wok about one-third full of vegetable oil. Heat to 190°C/375°F, or until a cube of bread browns in 30 seconds. Cook the rice cakes, 1 or 2 at a time, for 2–3 minutes until golden and crisp. Drain on absorbent kitchen paper. Serve with the mango salsa.

Try This: FOR AN ALTERNATIVE: 64   FOR A MORE SUBSTANTIAL OPTION: 250

Crispy Pancake Rolls

MAKES 8

250 g/9 oz plain flour
pinch of salt
1 medium egg
4 tsp sunflower oil
2 tbsp light olive oil
2 cm/¾ inch piece fresh root
    ginger, peeled and grated
1 garlic clove,
    peeled and crushed

225 g/8 oz tofu, drained and
    cut into small dice
2 tbsp soy sauce
1 tbsp dry sherry
175 g/6 oz button
    mushrooms, wiped
    and chopped
1 celery stalk, trimmed and
    finely chopped

2 spring onions, trimmed
    and finely chopped
2 tbsp groundnut oil
fresh coriander sprig and
    sliced spring onion,
    to garnish

Sift 225 g/8 oz of the flour with the salt into a large bowl, make a well in the centre and drop in the egg. Beat to form a smooth, thin batter, gradually adding 300 ml/½ pint of water and drawing in the flour from the sides of the bowl. Mix the remaining flour with 1–2 tablespoons of water to make a thick paste. Reserve.

Heat a little sunflower oil in a 20.5 cm/8 inch omelette or frying pan and pour in 2 tablespoons of the batter. Cook for 1–2 minutes, flip over and cook for a further 1–2 minutes, or until firm. Slide from the pan and keep warm. Make more pancakes with the remaining batter.

Heat a wok or large frying pan, add the olive oil and when hot, add the ginger, garlic and tofu, stir-fry for 30 seconds, then pour in the soy sauce and sherry. Add the mushrooms, celery and spring onions. Stir-fry for 1–2 minutes, then remove from the wok and leave to cool.

Place a little filling in the centre of each pancake. Brush the edges, with the flour paste, fold in the edges, then roll up into parcels. Heat the groundnut oil to 180°C/350°F in the wok. Fry the pancake rolls for 2–3 minutes or until golden. Serve immediately, garnished with chopped spring onions and a sprig of coriander.

Spring Rolls with Mixed Vegetables

MAKES 12

2 tbsp sesame oil
125 g/4 oz broccoli florets,
    cut into small pieces
125 g/4 oz carrots, peeled
    and cut into matchsticks
125 g/4 oz courgettes, cut
    into strips
150 g/5 oz button mushrooms,
    finely chopped

2.5 cm/1 inch piece fresh root
    ginger, peeled and grated
1 garlic clove, peeled and
    finely chopped
4 spring onions, trimmed
    and finely chopped
75 g/3 oz beansprouts
1 tbsp light soy sauce
pinch of cayenne pepper

4 tbsp plain flour
12 sheets filo pastry
300 ml/½ pint groundnut oil
spring onion curls,
    to garnish

Heat a wok, add the sesame oil and when hot, add the broccoli, carrots, courgettes, mushrooms, ginger, garlic and spring onions and stir-fry for 1–2 minutes, or until slightly softened.

Turn into a bowl, add the beansprouts, soy sauce and cayenne pepper and mix together. Transfer the vegetables to a colander and drain for 5 minutes. Meanwhile, blend the flour with 2–3 tablespoons of water to form a paste and reserve.

Fold a sheet of filo pastry in half and in half again, brushing a little water between each layer. Place a spoonful of the drained vegetable mixture on to the pastry. Brush a little of the flour paste along the edges. Turn the edges into the centre, then roll up and seal. Repeat with the rest.

Wipe the wok clean, return to the heat, add the oil and heat to 190°C/375°F. Add the spring rolls in batches and deep-fry for 2–3 minutes, or until golden. Drain on absorbent kitchen paper, arrange on a platter, garnish with spring onion curls and serve immediately.

Try This: FOR AN ALTERNATIVE: 68   FOR A MORE SUBSTANTIAL OPTION: 274

Olive & Feta Parcels

MAKES 6

1 small red pepper	125 g/4 oz feta cheese	3 tbsp olive oil
1 small yellow pepper	2 tbsp pine nuts, lightly	sour cream and chive dip,
125 g/4 oz marinated green	toasted	to serve
and black olives	6 sheets filo pastry	

Preheat the oven to 180°C/350°F/Gas Mark 4. Preheat the grill, then line the grill rack with tinfoil.

Cut the peppers into quarters and remove the seeds. Place skin side up on the foil-lined grill rack and cook under the preheated grill for 10 minutes, turning occasionally until the skins begin to blacken. Place the peppers in a polythene bag and leave until cool enough to handle, then skin and thinly slice.

Chop the olives and cut the feta cheese into small cubes. Mix together the olives, feta, sliced peppers and pine nuts.

Cut 1 sheet of filo pastry in half then brush with a little of the oil. Place a spoonful of the olive and feta mix about one third of the way up the pastry. Fold over the pastry and wrap to form a square parcel encasing the filling completely.

Place this parcel in the centre of the second half of the pastry sheet. Brush the edges lightly with a little oil, bring up the corners to meet in the centre and twist them loosely to form a purse. Brush with a little more oil and repeat with the remaining filo pastry and filling.

Place the parcels on a lightly oiled baking sheet and bake in the preheated oven for 10–15 minutes, or until crisp and golden brown. Serve with the dip.

Try This: FOR AN ALTERNATIVE: 74   FOR A MORE SUBSTANTIAL OPTION: 148

Mozzarella Parcels with Cranberry Relish

SERVES 6

125 g/4 oz mozzarella cheese
8 slices of thin white bread
2 medium eggs, beaten
salt and freshly ground
   black pepper

300 ml/1/2 pint olive oil

For the relish:
125 g/4 oz cranberries
2 tbsp fresh orange juice

grated rind of 1
   small orange
50 g/2 oz soft light
   brown sugar
1 tbsp port

Slice the mozzarella thinly, remove the crusts from the bread and make sandwiches with the bread and cheese. Cut into 5 cm/2 inch squares and squash them quite flat. Season the eggs with salt and pepper, then soak the bread in the seasoned egg for 1 minute on each side until well coated.

Heat the oil to 190°C/375°F and deep-fry the bread squares for 1–2 minutes, or until they are crisp and golden brown. Drain on absorbent kitchen paper and keep warm while the cranberry relish is prepared.

Place the cranberries, orange juice, rind, sugar and port into a small saucepan and add 5 tablespoons of water. Bring to the boil, then simmer for 10 minutes, or until the cranberries have 'popped'. Sweeten with a little more sugar if necessary.

Arrange the mozzarella parcels on individual serving plates. Serve with a little of the cranberry relish.

Try This: FOR AN ALTERNATIVE: 72   FOR A MORE SUBSTANTIAL OPTION: 124

Antipasti with Focaccia

SERVES 4

3 fresh figs, quartered
125 g/4 oz green beans,
   cooked and halved
1 small head of radicchio,
   rinsed and shredded
125 g/4 oz large prawns,
   peeled and cooked
125 can sardines, drained
25 g/1 oz pitted black olives

25 g/1 oz stuffed green olives
125 g/4 oz mozzarella
   cheese, sliced
50 g/2 oz Italian salami
   sausage, thinly sliced
3 tbsp olive oil
275 g/10 oz strong
   white flour
pinch of sugar

3 tsp easy-blend quick-
   acting yeast or 15 g/½ oz
   fresh yeast
175 g/6 oz fine semolina
1 tsp salt
300 ml/½ pint warm water
a little extra olive oil
   for brushing
1 tbsp coarse salt crystals

Preheat oven to 220°C/425°F/Gas Mark 7, 15 minutes before baking. Arrange the fresh fruit, vegetables, prawns, sardines, olives, cheese and meat on a large serving platter. Drizzle over 1 tablespoon of the olive oil, then cover and chill in the refrigerator while making the bread.

Sift the flour, sugar, semolina and salt into a large mixing bowl then sprinkle in the dried yeast. Make a well in the centre and add the remaining 2 tablespoons of olive oil. Add the warm water, a little at a time, and mix together until a smooth, pliable dough is formed. If using fresh yeast, cream the yeast with the sugar, then gradually beat in half the warm water. Leave in a warm place until frothy then proceed as for dried yeast.

Place on to a lightly floured board and knead until smooth and elastic. Place the dough in a lightly greased bowl, cover and leave in a warm place for 45 minutes.

Knead again and flatten the dough into a large, flat oval shape about 1 cm/½ inch thick. Place on a lightly oiled baking tray. Prick the surface with the end of a wooden spoon and brush with olive oil. Sprinkle on the coarse salt and bake in the preheated oven for 25 minutes, or until golden. Serve the bread with the prepared platter of food.

Try This: FOR AN ALTERNATIVE: 78   FOR A MORE SUBSTANTIAL OPTION: 100

Bruschetta with Pecorino, Garlic & Tomatoes

SERVES 4

6 ripe but firm tomatoes
125 g/4 oz pecorino cheese,
  finely grated
1 tbsp oregano leaves
salt and freshly ground

black pepper
3 tbsp olive oil
3 garlic cloves, peeled
8 slices of flat Italian bread,
  such as focaccia

50 g/2 oz mozzarella cheese
marinated black olives,
  to serve

Preheat grill and line the grill rack with tinfoil just before cooking. Make a small cross in the top of the tomatoes, then place in a small bowl and cover with boiling water. Leave to stand for 2 minutes, then drain and remove the skins. Cut into quarters, remove the seeds, and chop the flesh into small dice.

Mix the tomato flesh with the pecorino cheese and 2 teaspoons of the fresh oregano and season to taste with salt and pepper. Add 1 tablespoon of the olive oil and mix thoroughly.

Crush the garlic and spread evenly over the slices of bread. Heat 2 tablespoons of the olive oil in a large frying pan and sauté the bread slices until they are crisp and golden.

Place the fried bread on a lightly oiled baking tray and spoon on the tomato and cheese topping. Place a little mozzarella on top and place under the preheated grill for 3–4 minutes, until golden and bubbling. Garnish with the remaining oregano, then arrange the bruschettas on a serving plate and serve immediately with the olives.

Try This: FOR AN ALTERNATIVE: 76   FOR A MORE SUBSTANTIAL OPTION: 208

Roasted Aubergine Dip with Pitta Strips

SERVES 4

4 pitta breads
2 large aubergines
1 garlic clove, peeled
¼ tsp sesame oil

1 tbsp lemon juice
½ tsp ground cumin
salt and freshly ground
    black pepper

2 tbsp freshly
    chopped parsley
fresh salad leaves,
    to serve

Preheat the oven to 180°C/ 350°F/Gas Mark 4. On a chopping board cut the pitta breads into strips. Spread the bread in a single layer on to a large baking tray. Cook in the preheated oven for 15 minutes until golden and crisp. Leave to cool on a wire cooling rack.

Trim the aubergines, rinse lightly and reserve. Heat a griddle pan until almost smoking. Cook the aubergines and garlic for about 15 minutes. Turn the aubergines frequently, until very tender with wrinkled and charred skins. Remove from heat. Leave to cool.

When the aubergines are cool enough to handle, cut in half and scoop out the cooked flesh and place in a food processor. Squeeze the softened garlic flesh from the papery skin and add to the food processor.

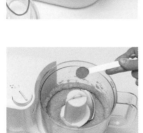

Blend the aubergine and garlic until smooth, then add the sesame oil, lemon juice and cumin and blend again to mix.

Season to taste with salt and pepper, stir in the parsley and serve with the pitta strips and mixed salad leaves.

Try This: FOR AN ALTERNATIVE: 82 FOR A MORE SUBSTANTIAL OPTION: 166

Sweet Potato Crisps
with Mango Salsa

SERVES 6

For the salsa:
1 large mango, peeled, stoned
   and cut into small cubes
8 cherry tomatoes, quartered
½ cucumber, peeled if
   preferred and finely diced
1 red onion, peeled and
   finely chopped
pinch of sugar
1 red chilli, deseeded and
   finely chopped
2 tbsp rice vinegar
2 tbsp olive oil
grated rind and juice of 1 lime

For the crisps:
450 g/1 lb sweet potatoes,
   peeled and thinly sliced
vegetable oil, for deep frying
sea salt
2 tbsp freshly chopped mint

To make the salsa, mix the mango with the tomatoes, cucumber and onion. Add the sugar, chilli, vinegar, oil and the lime rind and juice. Mix together thoroughly, cover and leave for 45–50 minutes.

Soak the potatoes in cold water for 40 minutes to remove as much of the excess starch as possible. Drain and dry thoroughly in a clean tea towel, or absorbent kitchen paper.

Heat the oil to 190°C/375°F in a deep fryer. When at the correct temperature, place half the potatoes in the frying basket, then carefully lower the potatoes into the hot oil and cook for 4–5 minutes, or until they are golden brown, shaking the basket every minute so that they do not stick together.

Drain the potato crisps on absorbent kitchen paper, sprinkle with sea salt and place under a preheated moderate grill for a few seconds to dry out. Repeat with the remaining potatoes.

Stir the mint into the salsa and serve with the potato crisps.

Try This: FOR AN ALTERNATIVE: 66   FOR A MORE SUBSTANTIAL OPTION: 90

Stuffed Vine Leaves

SERVES 6–8

150 g/5 oz long-grain rice
225 g/8 oz fresh or preserved vine leaves
225 g/8 oz red onion, peeled and finely chopped
3 baby leeks, trimmed and finely sliced
25 g/1 oz freshly chopped parsley
25 g/1 oz freshly chopped mint
25 g/1 oz freshly chopped dill
150 ml/¼ pint extra-virgin olive oil
salt and freshly ground black pepper
50 g/2 oz currants
50 g/2 oz ready-to-eat dried apricots, finely chopped
25 g/1 oz pine nuts
juice of 1 lemon
600–750 ml/1–1¼ pints boiling stock
lemon wedges or slices, to garnish
4 tbsp Greek-style yogurt, to serve

Soak the rice in cold water for 30 minutes. If using fresh vine leaves, blanch 5–6 leaves at a time in salted boiling water for a minute. Rinse and drain. If using preserved vine leaves, soak in tepid water for at least 20 minutes, drain, rinse and pat dry with absorbent kitchen paper.

Mix the onion and leeks with the herbs and half the oil. Add the drained rice, mix and season to taste with salt and pepper. Stir in the currants, apricots, pine nuts and lemon juice. Spoon 1 teaspoon of the filling on to the stalk end of each leaf. Roll, tucking the side flaps into the centre to create a neat parcel; do not roll too tight. Continue until all the filling is used.

Layer half the remaining vine leaves over the base of a large frying pan. Pack the little parcels in the frying pan and cover with the remaining leaves.

Pour in enough stock to just cover the vine leaves, add a pinch of salt and bring to the boil. Reduce the heat, cover and simmer for 45–55 minutes, or until the rice is sticky and tender. Leave to stand for 10 minutes. Drain the stock. Garnish with lemon wedges and serve hot with the Greek yogurt.

Try This: FOR AN ALTERNATIVE: 72   FOR A MORE SUBSTANTIAL OPTION: 260

Starters & Small Portions

Spicy Beef Pancakes

SERVES 4

50 g/2 oz plain flour
pinch of salt
½ tsp Chinese five
   spice powder
1 large egg yolk
150 ml/¼ pint milk
4 tsp sunflower oil
slices of spring onion,
   to garnish

For the spicy beef filling:
1 tbsp sesame oil
4 spring onions, sliced
1 cm/½ inch piece fresh root
   ginger, peeled and grated
1 garlic clove, peeled
   and crushed
300 g/11 oz sirloin steak,
   trimmed and cut into strips

1 red chilli, deseeded and
   finely chopped
1 tsp sherry vinegar
1 tsp soft dark brown sugar
1 tbsp dark soy sauce

Sift the flour, salt and Chinese five spice powder into a bowl and make a well in the centre. Add the egg yolk and a little of the milk. Gradually beat in, drawing in the flour to make a smooth batter. Whisk in the rest of the milk.

Heat 1 teaspoon of the sunflower oil in a small heavy-based frying pan. Pour in just enough batter to thinly coat the base of the pan. Cook over a medium heat for 1 minute, or until the underside of the pancake is golden brown. Turn or toss the pancake and cook for 1 minute, or until the other side of the pancake is golden brown. Make 7 more pancakes with the remaining batter. Stack them on a warmed plate as you make them, with greaseproof paper between each pancake. Cover with tinfoil and keep warm in a low oven.

Now make the filling. Heat a wok or large frying pan, add the sesame oil and, when hot, add the spring onions, ginger and garlic and stir-fry for 1 minute. Add the beef, stir-fry for 3–4 minutes, then stir in the chilli, vinegar, sugar and soy sauce. Cook for 1 minute, then remove from the heat.

Spoon one-eighth of the filling over one half of each pancake. Fold the pancakes in half, then fold in half again. Garnish with a few slices of spring onion and serve immediately.

Try This: FOR AN ALTERNATIVE: 156   FOR A MORE SUBSTANTIAL OPTION: 200

Sesame–coated Turkey with Mango Tabbouleh

SERVES 4

3 turkey breast fillets,
    about 450 g/1 lb, skinned
4 tbsp plain flour
4 tbsp sesame seeds
salt and freshly ground
    black pepper
1 medium egg, lightly
    beaten

2 tbsp sunflower oil

For the mango tabbouleh:
175 g/6 oz bulgar wheat
2 tbsp olive oil
juice of ½ lemon
6 spring onions, trimmed
    and finely chopped

1 red chilli, deseeded and
    finely chopped
1 ripe mango, peeled, pitted
    and diced
3 tbsp freshly
    chopped coriander
1 tbsp freshly chopped
    mint leaves

Cut the turkey across the grain into strips. Mix together the flour, sesame seeds, salt and pepper. Dip the turkey strips in the beaten egg, then in the sesame seed mixture to coat. Chill in the refrigerator until ready to cook.

For the tabbouleh, put the bulgar wheat in a large bowl and pour over plenty of boiling water. Cover the bowl with a plate and leave to soak for 20 minutes.

Whisk together the olive oil and lemon juice in a large bowl. Stir in the spring onions, chilli, mango, coriander and mint. Drain the bulgar and squeeze out any excess moisture with your hands, then add to the bowl, season to taste with salt and pepper and mix well.

Heat a wok, add the oil and, when hot, stir-fry the sesame-coated turkey strips in 2 batches for 4–5 minutes, or until golden, crispy and cooked through. Divide the turkey strips between individual serving plates and serve immediately with the tabbouleh.

Try This: FOR AN ALTERNATIVE: 66   FOR A MORE SUBSTANTIAL OPTION: 218

Griddled Garlic & Lemon Squid

SERVES 4

125 g/4 oz long-grain rice
300 ml/½ pint fish stock
225 g/8 oz squid, cleaned
finely grated rind of 1 lemon
1 garlic clove, peeled

and crushed
1 shallot, peeled and
  finely chopped
2 tbsp freshly
  chopped coriander

2 tbsp lemon juice
salt and freshly ground
  black pepper

Rinse the rice until the water runs clear, then place in a saucepan with the stock. Bring to the boil, then reduce the heat. Cover and simmer gently for 10 minutes. Turn off the heat and leave the pan covered so the rice can steam while you cook the squid.

Remove the tentacles from the squid and reserve. Cut the body cavity in half. Using the tip of a small sharp knife, score the inside flesh of the body cavity in a diamond pattern. Do not cut all the way through.

Mix the lemon rind, crushed garlic and chopped shallot together.

Place the squid in a shallow bowl and sprinkle over the lemon mixture and stir.

Heat a griddle pan until almost smoking. Cook the squid for 3–4 minutes until cooked through, then slice.

Sprinkle with the coriander and lemon juice. Season to taste with salt and pepper. Drain the rice and serve immediately with the squid.

Try This: FOR AN ALTERNATIVE: 106   FOR A MORE SUBSTANTIAL OPTION: 226

Salmon Fish Cakes

SERVES 4

225 g/8 oz potatoes, peeled
450 g/1 lb salmon
   fillet, skinned
125 g/4 oz carrot, trimmed
   and peeled
2 tbsp grated lemon rind

2–3 tbsp freshly
   chopped coriander
1 medium egg yolk
salt and freshly ground
   black pepper
2 tbsp plain white flour

few fine sprays of oil

To serve:
prepared tomato sauce
tossed green salad
crusty bread

Cube the potatoes and cook in lightly salted boiling water for 15 minutes. Drain and mash the potatoes. Place in a mixing bowl and reserve.

Place the salmon in a food processor and blend to form a chunky purée. Add the purée to the potatoes and mix together. Coarsely grate the carrot and add to the fish mixture with the lemon rind and the coriander.

Add the egg yolk, season to taste with salt and pepper, then gently mix the ingredients together. With damp hands form the mixture into 4 large fish cakes. Coat in the flour and place on a plate. Cover loosely and chill for at least 30 minutes.

When ready to cook, spray a griddle pan with a few fine sprays of oil and heat the pan. When hot add the fish cakes and cook on both sides for 3–4 minutes or until the fish is cooked. Add an extra spray of oil if needed during the cooking.

When the fish cakes are cooked, serve immediately with the tomato sauce, green salad and crusty bread.

Try This: FOR AN ALTERNATIVE: 96 FOR A MORE SUBSTANTIAL OPTION: 230

Creamy Salmon with Dill in Filo Baskets

SERVES 4

1 bay leaf
6 black peppercorns
1 large sprig fresh parsley
175 g/6 oz salmon fillet

4 large sheets filo pastry
fine spray of oil
125 g/4 oz baby spinach leaves
8 tbsp low-fat fromage frais

2 tsp Dijon mustard
2 tbsp freshly chopped dill
salt and freshly ground
　black pepper

Preheat the oven to 200˚C/400˚F/Gas Mark 6. Place the bay leaf, peppercorns, parsley and salmon in a frying pan and add enough water to barely cover the fish. Bring to the boil, reduce the heat and poach the fish for 5 minutes until it flakes easily. Remove it from the pan. Reserve.

Spray each sheet of filo pastry lightly with the oil. Scrunch up the pastry to make a nest shape approximately 12.5 cm/5 inches in diameter. Place on a lightly oiled baking sheet and cook in the preheated oven for 10 minutes until golden and crisp.

Blanch the spinach in a pan of lightly salted boiling water for 2 minutes. Drain thoroughly and keep warm.

Mix the fromage frais, mustard and dill together, then warm gently. Season to taste with salt and pepper. Divide the spinach between the filo pastry nests and flake the salmon on to the spinach.

Spoon the mustard and dill sauce over the filo baskets and serve immediately.

Try This: FOR AN ALTERNATIVE: 98　FOR A MORE SUBSTANTIAL OPTION: 228

Salmon & Roasted Red Pepper Pasta

SERVES 6

225 g/8 oz skinless and
  boneless salmon fillet,
  thinly sliced
3 shallots, peeled and
  finely chopped
1 tbsp freshly
  chopped parsley

6 tbsp olive oil
juice of ½ lemon
2 red peppers, deseeded
  and quartered
handful fresh basil leaves,
  shredded
50 g/2 oz fresh breadcrumbs

4 tbsp extra virgin olive oil
450 g/1 lb fettuccine
  or linguine
6 spring onions, trimmed
  and shredded
salt and freshly ground
  black pepper

Preheat the grill to high. Place the salmon in a bowl. Add the shallots, parsley, 3 tablespoons of the olive oil and the lemon juice. Reserve.

Brush the pepper quarters with a little olive oil. Cook them under the preheated grill for 8–10 minutes, or until the skins have blackened and the flesh is tender. Place the peppers in a plastic bag until cool enough to handle. When cooled, peel the peppers and cut into strips. Put the strips into a bowl with the basil and the remaining olive oil and reserve.

Toast the breadcrumbs until dry and lightly browned then toss with the extra virgin olive oil and reserve.

Bring a large pan of salted water to a rolling boil and add the pasta. Cook according to the packet instructions, or until 'al dente'.

Meanwhile, transfer the peppers and their marinade to a hot frying pan. Add the spring onions and cook for 1–2 minutes, or until they have just softened. Add the salmon and its marinade and cook for a further 1–2 minutes, or until the salmon is just cooked. Season to taste with salt and pepper. Drain the pasta thoroughly and transfer to a warmed serving bowl. Add the salmon mixture and toss gently. Garnish with the breadcrumbs and serve immediately.

Try This: FOR AN ALTERNATIVE: 108   FOR A MORE SUBSTANTIAL OPTION: 232

Fried Whitebait
with Rocket Salad

SERVES 4

450 g/1 lb whitebait,
   fresh or frozen
oil, for frying
85 g/3 oz plain flour
½ tsp of cayenne pepper
salt and freshly ground
   black pepper

For the salad:
125 g/4 oz rocket leaves
125 g/4 oz cherry tomatoes,
   halved
75 g/3 oz cucumber,
   cut into dice
3 tbsp olive oil

1 tbsp fresh lemon juice
½ tsp Dijon mustard
½ tsp caster sugar

If the whitebait are frozen, thaw completely, then wipe dry with absorbent kitchen paper.

Start to heat the oil in a deep-fat fryer. Arrange the fish in a large, shallow dish and toss well in the flour, cayenne pepper and salt and pepper.

Deep fry the fish in batches for 2–3 minutes, or until crisp and golden. Keep the cooked fish warm while deep frying the remaining fish.

Meanwhile, to make the salad, arrange the rocket leaves, cherry tomatoes and cucumber on individual serving dishes. Whisk the olive oil and the remaining ingredients together and season lightly. Drizzle the dressing over the salad and serve with the whitebait.

Try This: FOR AN ALTERNATIVE: 102   FOR A MORE SUBSTANTIAL OPTION: 244

Prawn Salad
with Toasted Rice

SERVES 4

For the dressing:
50 ml/2 fl oz rice vinegar
1 red chilli, deseeded and
   thinly sliced
7.5 cm/3 inch piece lemon
   grass stalk, bruised
juice of 1 lime
2 tbsp Thai fish sauce
1 tsp sugar, or to taste

For the salad:
350 g/12 oz large raw
   prawns, peeled with tails
   attached, heads removed
cayenne pepper
1 tbsp long-grain white rice
salt and freshly ground
   black pepper
2 tbsp sunflower oil

1 large head Chinese leaves
   or cos lettuce, shredded
½ small cucumber,
   peeled, deseeded and
   thinly sliced
1 small bunch chives, cut
   into 2.5 cm/1 inch pieces
small bunch of mint leaves

Place all the ingredients for the dressing in a small bowl and leave to stand to let the flavours blend together.

Using a sharp knife, split each prawn lengthways in half, leaving the tail attached to one half. Remove any black vein and pat the prawns dry with absorbent kitchen paper. Sprinkle the prawns with a little salt and cayenne pepper and then reserve.

Heat a wok over a high heat. Add the rice and stir-fry until browned and fragrant. Turn into a mortar and cool. Crush gently with a pestle until coarse crumbs form. Wipe the wok clean.

Reheat the wok, add the oil and when hot, add the prawns and stir-fry for 2 minutes, or until pink. Transfer to a plate and season to taste with salt and pepper.

Place the Chinese leaves or lettuce into a salad bowl with the cucumber, chives and mint leaves and toss lightly together. Remove the lemon grass stalk and some of the chilli from the dressing and pour all but 2 tablespoons over the salad and toss until lightly coated. Add the prawns and drizzle with the remaining dressing, then sprinkle with the toasted rice and serve.

Try This: FOR AN ALTERNATIVE: 44   FOR A MORE SUBSTANTIAL OPTION: 224

Louisiana Prawns & Fettuccine

SERVES 4

4 tbsp olive oil
450 g/1 lb raw tiger prawns, washed and peeled, shells and heads reserved
2 shallots, peeled and finely chopped
4 garlic cloves, peeled and finely chopped
large handful fresh

basil leaves
1 carrot, peeled and finely chopped
1 onion, peeled and finely chopped
1 celery stick, trimmed and finely chopped
2–3 sprigs fresh parsley
2–3 sprigs fresh thyme

salt and freshly ground black pepper
pinch cayenne pepper
175 ml/6 fl oz dry white wine
450 g/1 lb ripe tomatoes, roughly chopped
juice of ½ lemon, or to taste
350 g/12 oz fettuccine

Heat half the oil in a large saucepan and add the prawn shells and heads. Fry on high for 2–3 minutes, until the shells turn pink and lightly browned. Add half the shallots, garlic and basil, and the carrot, onion, celery, parsley and thyme. Season with salt, pepper and cayenne and sauté for 2–3 minutes, stirring often. Pour in the wine and stir. Bring to the boil and simmer for 1 minute, then add the tomatoes. Cook for a further 3–4 minutes then pour in 200 ml/7 fl oz water. Bring to the boil, then simmer for about 30 minutes, stirring often and using a wooden spoon to mash the prawn shells in order to release as much flavour as possible. Lower the heat if the sauce is reducing very quickly.

Strain through a sieve, pressing well to extract as much liquid as possible; there should be about 450 ml/¾ pint. Pour the liquid into a clean pan and bring to the boil, then lower the heat and simmer gently until the liquid is reduced by about half. Heat the remaining olive oil over a high heat in a clean frying pan and add the peeled prawns. Season lightly and add the lemon juice. Cook for 1 minute, lower the heat and add the remaining shallots and garlic. Cook for 1 minute. Add the sauce and adjust the seasoning. Meanwhile, bring a large pan of lightly salted water to a rolling boil and add the fettuccine. Cook according to the packet instructions, or until 'al dente', and drain thoroughly. Transfer to a warmed serving dish. Add the sauce and toss well. Garnish with the remaining basil and serve immediately.

Try This: FOR AN ALTERNATIVE: 102   FOR A MORE SUBSTANTIAL OPTION: 226

Mussels with Creamy Garlic & Saffron Sauce

SERVES 4

700 g/1½ lb fresh live mussels
300 ml/½ pint good-quality
   dry white wine
1 tbsp olive oil
1 shallot, peeled and

finely chopped
2 garlic cloves, peeled
   and crushed
1 tbsp freshly
   chopped oregano

2 saffron strands
150 ml/¼ pint single cream
salt and freshly ground
   black pepper
fresh crusty bread, to serve

Clean the mussels thoroughly in plenty of cold water and remove any beards and barnacles from the shells. Discard any mussels that are open or damaged. Place in a large bowl and cover with cold water and leave in the refrigerator until required, if prepared earlier.

Pour the wine into a large saucepan and bring to the boil. Tip the mussels into the pan, cover and cook, shaking the saucepan periodically for 6–8 minutes, or until the mussels have opened completely.

Discard any mussels with closed shells, then, using a slotted spoon, carefully remove the remaining open mussels from the saucepan and keep them warm. Reserve the cooking liquor.

Heat the olive oil in a small frying pan and cook the shallot and garlic gently for 2–3 minutes, until softened. Add the reserved cooking liquid and chopped oregano and cook for a further 3–4 minutes. Stir in the saffron and the cream and heat through gently. Season to taste with salt and pepper. Place a few mussels in individual serving bowls and spoon over the saffron sauce. Serve immediately with plenty of fresh crusty bread.

Try This: FOR AN ALTERNATIVE: 96   FOR A MORE SUBSTANTIAL OPTION: 236

Linguine with Fennel, Crab & Chervil

SERVES 6

450g/1 lb linguine
25 g/1 oz butter
2 carrots, peeled
   and finely diced
2 shallots, peeled and
   finely diced
2 celery sticks, trimmed

and finely diced
1 bulb fennel, trimmed
   and finely diced
6 spring onions, trimmed
   and finely chopped
300 ml/½ pint double cream
3 tbsp freshly chopped

chervil, plus extra for
   garnish
1 large cooked crab
salt and freshly ground
   pepper
juice of ½ lemon, or to taste
sprig of dill, to garnish

Bring a large pan of lightly salted water to a rolling boil. Add the pasta and cook according to the packet instructions, or until 'al dente'.

Meanwhile, heat the butter in a large saucepan. Add the carrots, shallots, celery, fennel and three-quarters of the chopped spring onions. Cook the vegetables gently for 8–10 minutes, or until tender, stirring frequently and ensuring that they do not brown.

Add the double cream and chopped chervil to the vegetable mixture. Scrape the crab meat over the sauce, then stir to mix the sauce ingredients.

Season the sauce to taste with salt and pepper and stir in the lemon juice. Drain the pasta thoroughly and transfer to a large warmed serving dish. Pour over the sauce and toss. Garnish with extra chervil, the remaining spring onions and a sprig of dill. Serve immediately.

Try This: FOR AN ALTERNATIVE: 52   FOR A MORE SUBSTANTIAL OPTION: 248

Fusilli with Spicy Tomato & Chorizo Sauce with Roasted Peppers

4 tbsp olive oil
1 red pepper, deseeded
   and quartered
1 yellow pepper, deseeded
   and quartered
175 g/6 oz chorizo (outer
   skin removed),

roughly chopped
2 garlic cloves, peeled and
   finely chopped
large pinch chilli flakes
700 g/1½ lb ripe tomatoes,
   skinned and roughly
   chopped

salt and freshly ground
   black pepper
450 g/1 lb fusilli
basil leaves, to garnish
freshly grated Parmesan
   cheese, to serve

Preheat the grill to high. Brush the pepper quarters with 1 tablespoon of the olive oil, then cook under the preheated grill, turning once, for 8–10 minutes, or until the skins have blackened and the flesh is tender. Place the peppers in a plastic bag until cool enough to handle. When cooled, peel the peppers, slice very thinly and reserve.

Heat the remaining oil in a frying pan and add the chorizo. Cook over a medium heat for 3–4 minutes, or until starting to brown. Add the garlic and chilli flakes and cook for a further 2–3 minutes.

Add the tomatoes, season lightly with salt and pepper then cook gently for about 5 minutes, or until the tomatoes have broken down. Lower the heat and cook for a further 10–15 minutes, or until the sauce has thickened. Add the peppers and heat gently for 1-2 minutes. Adjust the seasoning to taste.

Meanwhile, bring a large pan of lightly salted water to a rolling boil. Add the fusilli and cook according to the packet instructions, or until 'al dente'. Drain thoroughly and transfer to a warmed serving dish. Pour over the sauce, sprinkle with basil and serve with Parmesan cheese.

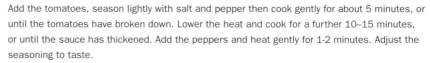

Try This: FOR AN ALTERNATIVE: 112   FOR A MORE SUBSTANTIAL OPTION: 268

Fettuccine with Wild Mushrooms & Prosciutto

SERVES 6

15 g/½ oz dried porcini mushrooms
150 ml/¼ pint hot chicken stock
2 tbsp olive oil
1 small onion, peeled and finely chopped
2 garlic cloves, peeled and finely chopped
4 slices prosciutto, chopped or torn
225 g/8 oz mixed wild or cultivated mushrooms, wiped and sliced if necessary
450 g/1 lb fettuccine
3 tbsp crème fraîche
2 tbsp freshly chopped parsley
salt and freshly ground black pepper
freshly grated Parmesan cheese, to serve (optional)

Place the dried mushrooms in a small bowl and pour over the hot chicken stock. Leave to soak for 15–20 minutes, or until the mushrooms have softened.

Meanwhile, heat the olive oil in a large frying pan. Add the onion and cook for 5 minutes over a medium heat, or until softened. Add the garlic and cook for 1 minute, then add the prosciutto and cook for a further minute.

Drain the dried mushrooms, reserving the soaking liquid. Roughly chop and add to the frying pan together with the fresh mushrooms. Cook over a high heat for 5 minutes, stirring often, or until softened. Strain the mushroom soaking liquid into the pan.

Meanwhile, bring a large pan of lightly salted water to a rolling boil. Add the pasta and cook according to the packet instructions, or until 'al dente'.

Stir the crème fraîche and chopped parsley into the mushroom mixture and heat through gently. Season to taste with salt and pepper. Drain the pasta well, transfer to a large warmed serving dish and pour over the sauce. Serve immediately with grated Parmesan cheese.

Try This: FOR AN ALTERNATIVE: 116   FOR A MORE SUBSTANTIAL OPTION: 202

Gnocchetti with Broccoli & Bacon Sauce

SERVES 6

450 g/1 lb broccoli florets
4 tbsp olive oil
50 g/2 oz pancetta or smoked
   bacon, finely chopped
1 small onion, peeled and
   finely chopped

3 garlic cloves, peeled
   and sliced
200 ml/7 fl oz milk
450 g/1 lb gnocchetti (little
   elongated ribbed shells)
50 g/2 oz freshly grated

Parmesan cheese,
   plus extra to serve
salt and freshly ground
   black pepper

Bring a large pan of salted water to the boil. Add the broccoli florets and cook for about 8–10 minutes, or until very soft. Drain thoroughly, allow to cool slightly then chop finely and reserve.

Heat the olive oil in a heavy-based pan, add the pancetta or bacon and cook over a medium heat for 5 minutes, or until golden and crisp. Add the onion and cook for a further 5 minutes, or until soft and lightly golden. Add the garlic and cook for 1 minute.

Transfer the chopped broccoli to the bacon or pancetta mixture and pour in the milk. Bring slowly to the boil and simmer rapidly for about 15 minutes, or until reduced to a creamy texture.

Meanwhile, bring a large pan of lightly salted water to a rolling boil. Add the pasta and cook according to the packet instructions, or until 'al dente'.

Drain the pasta thoroughly, reserving a little of the cooking water. Add the pasta and the Parmesan cheese to the broccoli mixture. Toss, adding enough of the reserved cooking water to make a creamy sauce. Season to taste with salt and pepper. Serve immediately with extra Parmesan cheese.

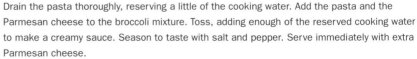

Try This: FOR AN ALTERNATIVE: 116   FOR A MORE SUBSTANTIAL OPTION: 256

Penne with Artichokes, Bacon & Mushrooms

SERVES 6

2 tbsp olive oil
75 g/3 oz smoked bacon or
  pancetta, chopped
1 small onion, peeled and
  finely sliced
125 g/4 oz chestnut
  mushrooms, wiped
  and sliced
2 garlic cloves, peeled

and finely chopped
400 g/14 oz can artichoke
  hearts, drained and halved,
  or quartered if large
100 ml/3½ fl oz dry
  white wine
100 ml/3½ fl oz
  chicken stock
3 tbsp double cream

50 g/2 oz freshly grated
  Parmesan cheese,
  plus extra to serve
salt and freshly ground
  black pepper
450 g/1 lb penne
shredded basil leaves,
  to garnish

Heat the olive oil in a frying pan and add the pancetta or bacon and the onion. Cook over a medium heat for 8–10 minutes, or until the bacon is crisp and the onion is just golden. Add the mushrooms and garlic and cook for a further 5 minutes, or until softened.

Add the artichoke hearts to the mushroom mixture and cook for 3–4 minutes. Pour in the wine, bring to the boil then simmer rapidly until the liquid is reduced and syrupy.

Pour in the chicken stock, bring to the boil then simmer rapidly for about 5 minutes, or until slightly reduced. Reduce the heat slightly, then slowly stir in the double cream and Parmesan cheese. Season the sauce to taste with salt and pepper.

Meanwhile, bring a large pan of lightly salted water to a rolling boil. Add the pasta and cook according to the packet instructions, or until 'al dente'.

Drain the pasta thoroughly and transfer to a large warmed serving dish. Pour over the sauce and toss together. Garnish with shredded basil and serve with extra Parmesan cheese.

Try This: FOR AN ALTERNATIVE: 120   FOR A MORE SUBSTANTIAL OPTION: 234

Italian Baked Tomatoes with Curly Endive & Radicchio

SERVES 4

1 tsp olive oil
4 beef tomatoes
salt
50 g/2 oz fresh white
  breadcrumbs
1 tbsp freshly snipped chives
1 tbsp freshly chopped parsley

125 g/4 oz button
  mushrooms,
  finely chopped
salt and freshly ground black
  pepper
25 g/1 oz fresh Parmesan
  cheese, grated

For the salad:
½ curly endive lettuce
½ small piece of radicchio
2 tbsp olive oil
1 tsp balsamic vinegar
salt and freshly ground
  black pepper

Preheat oven to 190˚C/375˚F/Gas Mark 5. Lightly oil a baking tray with the teaspoon of oil. Slice the tops off the tomatoes and remove all the tomato flesh and sieve into a large bowl. Sprinkle a little salt inside the tomato shells and then place them upside down on a plate while the filling is prepared.

Mix the sieved tomato with the breadcrumbs, fresh herbs and mushrooms and season well with salt and pepper. Place the tomato shells on the prepared baking tray and fill with the tomato and mushroom mixture. Sprinkle the cheese on the top and bake in the preheated oven for 15–20 minutes, until golden brown.

Meanwhile, prepare the salad. Arrange the endive and radicchio on individual serving plates and mix the remaining ingredients together in a small bowl to make the dressing. Season to taste.

When the tomatoes are cooked, allow to rest for 5 minutes, then place on the prepared plates and drizzle over a little dressing. Serve warm.

Try This: FOR AN ALTERNATIVE: 178   FOR A MORE SUBSTANTIAL OPTION: 208

Spaghettini with Lemon Pesto & Cheese & Herb Bread

SERVES 4

1 small onion,
    peeled and grated
2 tsp freshly
    chopped oregano
1 tbsp freshly
    chopped parsley
75 g/3 oz butter
125 g/4 oz pecorino cheese,

grated
8 slices of Italian flat bread
275 g/10 oz dried spaghettini
4 tbsp olive oil
1 large bunch of basil,
    approximately 30 g/1 oz
75 g/3 oz pine nuts
1 garlic clove,

peeled and crushed
75 g/3 oz Parmesan cheese,
    grated
finely grated rind and juice
    of 2 lemons
salt and freshly ground
    black pepper
4 tsp butter

Preheat oven to 200°C/400°F/Gas Mark 6, 15 minutes before baking. Mix together the onion, oregano, parsley, butter and cheese. Spread the bread with the cheese mixture, place on a lightly oiled baking tray and cover with tinfoil. Bake in the preheated oven for 10–15 minutes, then keep warm.

Add the spaghettini with 1 tablespoon of olive oil to a large saucepan of fast-boiling, lightly salted water and cook for 3–4 minutes, or until 'al dente'. Drain, reserving 2 tablespoons of the cooking liquor.

Blend the basil, pine nuts, garlic, Parmesan cheese, lemon rind and juice and remaining olive oil in a food processor or blender until a purée is formed. Season to taste with salt and pepper, then place in a saucepan.

Heat the lemon pesto very gently until piping hot, then stir in the pasta together with the reserved cooking liquor. Add the butter and mix well together.

Add plenty of black pepper to the pasta and serve immediately with the warm cheese and herb bread.

Try This: FOR AN ALTERNATIVE: 138   FOR A MORE SUBSTANTIAL OPTION: 270

Peperonata
(Braised Mixed Peppers)

SERVES 4

2 green peppers
1 red pepper
1 yellow pepper
1 orange pepper
1 onion, peeled
2 garlic cloves, peeled

2 tbsp olive oil
4 very ripe tomatoes
1 tbsp freshly
   chopped oregano
salt and freshly ground
   black pepper

150 ml/¼ pint light chicken
   or vegetable stock
sprigs of fresh oregano,
   to garnish
focaccia (*see* recipe page 76)
   or flat bread, to serve

Remove the seeds from the peppers and cut into thin strips. Slice the onion into rings and chop the garlic cloves finely.

Heat the olive oil in a frying pan and fry the peppers, onions and garlic for 5–10 minutes, or until soft and lightly coloured. Stir continuously.

Make a cross on the top of the tomatoes then place in a bowl and cover with boiling water. Allow to stand for about 2 minutes. Drain, then remove the skins and seeds and chop the tomato flesh into cubes.

Add the tomatoes and oregano to the peppers and onion and season to taste with salt and pepper. Cover the pan and bring to the boil. Simmer gently for about 30 minutes, or until tender, adding the chicken or vegetable stock halfway through the cooking time.

Garnish with sprigs of oregano and serve hot with plenty of freshly baked focaccia bread or alternatively lightly toast slices of flat bread and pile a spoonful of peperonata on to each plate.

Try This: FOR AN ALTERNATIVE: 180   FOR A MORE SUBSTANTIAL OPTION: 260

Mozzarella Frittata
with Tomato & Basil Salad

SERVES 6

For the salad:
6 ripe but firm tomatoes
2 tbsp fresh basil leaves
2 tbsp olive oil
1 tbsp fresh lemon juice
1 tsp caster sugar

freshly ground black pepper

For the frittata:
7 medium eggs, beaten
salt
300 g/11 oz mozzarella cheese

2 spring onions, trimmed
and finely chopped
2 tbsp olive oil
warm crusty bread, to serve

To make the tomato and basil salad, slice the tomatoes very thinly, tear up the basil leaves and sprinkle over. Make the dressing by whisking the olive oil, lemon juice and sugar together well. Season with black pepper before drizzling the dressing over the salad.

To make the frittata, preheat the grill to a high heat, just before beginning to cook. Place the eggs in a large bowl with plenty of salt and whisk. Grate the mozzarella and stir into the egg with the finely chopped spring onions.

Heat the oil in a large, non-stick frying pan and pour in the egg mixture, stirring with a wooden spoon to spread the ingredients evenly over the pan.

Cook for 5–8 minutes, until the frittata is golden brown and firm on the underside. Place the whole pan under the preheated grill and cook for about 4–5 minutes, or until the top is golden brown. Slide the frittata on to a serving plate, cut into 6 large wedges and serve immediately with the tomato and basil salad and plenty of warm crusty bread.

Try This: FOR AN ALTERNATIVE: 74   FOR A MORE SUBSTANTIAL OPTION: 208

Fresh Tagliatelle with Courgettes

SERVES 4–6

225 g /8 oz strong plain
    bread flour or type 00
    pasta flour, plus extra
    for rolling
1 tsp salt
2 medium eggs
1 medium egg yolk

3 tbsp extra virgin olive oil
2 small courgettes, halved
    lengthwise and thinly
    sliced
2 garlic cloves, peeled and
    thinly sliced
large pinch chilli flakes

zest of ½ lemon
1 tbsp freshly shredded basil
salt and freshly ground
    black pepper
freshly grated Parmesan
    cheese, to serve

Sift the flour and salt into a large bowl, make a well in the centre and add the eggs and yolk, 1 tablespoon of oil and 1 teaspoon of water. Gradually mix to form a soft but not sticky dough, adding a little more flour or water as necessary. Turn out on to a lightly floured surface and knead for 5 minutes, or until smooth and elastic. Wrap in clingfilm and leave to rest at room temperature for about 30 minutes. Divide the dough into 8 pieces. Feed a piece of dough through a pasta machine. Gradually decrease the settings on the rollers, feeding the pasta through each time, until the sheet is very long and thin. If the pasta seems sticky, dust the work surface and both sides of the pasta generously with flour. Cut in half crosswise and hang over a clean pole. Repeat with the remaining dough. Leave to dry for about 5 minutes. Feed each sheet through the tagliatelle cutter, hanging the cut pasta over the pole. Leave to dry for a further 5 minutes. Wind a handful of pasta strands into nests and leave on a floured tea towel. Repeat with the remaining dough and leave to dry for 5 minutes.

Cook the pasta in plenty of salted boiling water for 2–3 minutes, or until 'al dente'. Meanwhile, heat the remaining oil in a large frying pan and add the courgettes, garlic, chilli and lemon zest. Cook over a medium heat for 3–4 minutes, or until the courgettes are lightly golden and tender. Drain the pasta thoroughly, reserving 2 tablespoons of the cooking water. Add the pasta to the courgettes with the basil and seasoning. Mix well, adding the reserved cooking water. Serve with the Parmesan cheese.

Try This: FOR AN ALTERNATIVE: 136   FOR A MORE SUBSTANTIAL OPTION: 268

Beetroot Ravioli with Dill Cream Sauce

SERVES 4–6

fresh pasta (*see* Fresh
  Tagliatelle with
  Courgettes, page 126)
1 tbsp olive oil
1 small onion, peeled and
  finely chopped
½ tsp caraway seeds
175 g/6 oz cooked

beetroot, chopped
175 g/6 oz ricotta cheese
25 g/1 oz fresh white
  breadcrumbs
1 medium egg yolk
2 tbsp grated Parmesan
  cheese
salt and freshly ground

black pepper
4 tbsp walnut oil
4 tbsp freshly chopped dill
1 tbsp green peppercorns,
  drained and roughly
  chopped
6 tbsp crème fraîche

Make the pasta dough according to the recipe on page 126. Wrap in clingfilm and leave to rest for 30 minutes.

Heat the olive oil in a large frying pan, add the onion and caraway seeds and cook over a medium heat for 5 minutes, or until the onion is softened and lightly golden. Stir in the beetroot and cook for 5 minutes. Blend the beetroot mixture in a food processor until smooth, then allow to cool. Stir in the ricotta cheese, breadcrumbs, egg yolk and Parmesan cheese. Season the filling to taste with salt and pepper and reserve.

Divide the pasta dough into 8 pieces. Roll out as for tagliatelle, but do not cut the sheets in half. Lay 1 sheet on a floured surface and place 5 heaped teaspoons of the filling 2.5 cm/1 inch apart. Dampen around the heaps of filling and lay a second sheet of pasta over the top. Press around the heaps to seal. Cut into squares using a pastry wheel or sharp knife. Put the filled pasta shapes on to a floured tea towel.

Bring a pan of lightly salted water to a rolling boil. Drop in the ravioli, return to the boil and cook for 3–4 minutes, or until 'al dente'. Meanwhile, heat the walnut oil in a small pan then add the chopped dill and green peppercorns. Remove from the heat, stir in the crème fraîche and season well. Drain the cooked pasta and toss with the sauce. Serve immediately in warmed dishes.

Try This: FOR AN ALTERNATIVE: 130   FOR A MORE SUBSTANTIAL OPTION: 258

Beetroot Risotto

SERVES 6

6 tbsp extra-virgin olive oil
1 onion, peeled and
   finely chopped
2 garlic cloves, peeled and
   finely chopped
2 tsp freshly chopped thyme
1 tsp grated lemon rind
350 g/12 oz Arborio rice

150 ml/¼ pint dry
   white wine
900 ml/1½ pints vegetable
   stock, heated
2 tbsp double cream
225 g/8 oz cooked beetroot,
   peeled and finely chopped
2 tbsp freshly

chopped parsley
75 g/3 oz Parmesan cheese,
   freshly grated
salt and freshly ground
   black pepper
sprigs of fresh thyme,
   to garnish

Heat half the oil in a large heavy-based frying pan. Add the onion, garlic, thyme and lemon rind. Cook for 5 minutes, stirring frequently, until the onion is soft and transparent but not coloured. Add the rice and stir until it is well coated in the oil.

Add the wine, then bring to the boil and boil rapidly until the wine has almost evaporated. Reduce the heat.

Keeping the pan over a low heat, add a ladleful of the hot stock to the rice and cook, stirring constantly, until the stock is absorbed. Continue gradually adding the stock in this way until the rice is tender; this should take about 20 minutes. You may not need all the stock.

Stir in the cream, chopped beetroot, parsley and half the grated Parmesan cheese. Season to taste with salt and pepper. Garnish with sprigs of fresh thyme and serve immediately with the remaining grated Parmesan cheese.

Try This: FOR AN ALTERNATIVE: 128   FOR A MORE SUBSTANTIAL OPTION: 282

Gnocchi with Grilled Cherry Tomato Sauce

SERVES 4

450 g/1 lb floury potatoes, unpeeled
1 medium egg
1 tsp salt
75–90 g/3–3½ oz plain flour
450 g/1 lb mixed red and orange cherry tomatoes,

halved lengthways
2 garlic cloves, peeled and finely sliced
zest of ½ lemon, finely grated
1 tbsp freshly chopped thyme
1 tbsp freshly chopped basil

2 tbsp extra virgin olive oil, plus extra for drizzling
salt and freshly ground black pepper
pinch of sugar
freshly grated Parmesan cheese, to serve

Preheat the grill just before required. Bring a large pan of salted water to the boil, add the potatoes and cook for 20–25 minutes until tender. Drain. Leave until cool enough to handle but still hot, then peel them and place in a large bowl. Mash until smooth then work in the egg, salt and enough of the flour to form a soft dough.

With floured hands, roll a spoonful of the dough into a small ball. Flatten the ball slightly on to the back of a large fork, then roll it off the fork to make a little ridged dumpling. Place each gnocchi on to a floured tea towel as you work.

Place the tomatoes in a flameproof shallow dish. Add the garlic, lemon zest, herbs and olive oil. Season to taste with salt and pepper and sprinkle over the sugar. Cook under the preheated grill for 10 minutes, or until the tomatoes are charred and tender, stirring once or twice.

Meanwhile, bring a large pan of lightly salted water to the boil then reduce to a steady simmer. Dropping in 6–8 gnocchi at a time, cook in batches for 3–4 minutes, or until they begin bobbing up to the surface. Remove with a slotted spoon and drain well on absorbent kitchen paper before transferring to a warmed serving dish; cover with foil. Toss the cooked gnocchi with the tomato sauce. Serve immediately with a little grated Parmesan cheese.

Try This: FOR AN ALTERNATIVE: 134 FOR A MORE SUBSTANTIAL OPTION: 268

Spinach & Ricotta Gnocchi with Butter & Parmesan

SERVES 2–4

125 g/4 oz frozen leaf
   spinach, thawed
225 g/8 oz ricotta cheese
2 small eggs, lightly beaten
50 g/2 oz freshly grated

Parmesan cheese
salt and freshly ground
   black pepper
2 tbsp freshly chopped basil
50 g/2 oz plain flour

50 g/2 oz unsalted butter
2 garlic cloves, peeled
   and crushed
Parmesan cheese shavings,
   to serve

Squeeze the excess moisture from the spinach and chop finely. Blend in a food processor with the ricotta cheese, eggs, Parmesan cheese, seasoning and 1 tablespoon of the basil until smooth. Scrape into a bowl then add sufficient flour to form a soft, slightly sticky dough.

Bring a large pan of salted water to a rolling boil. Transfer the spinach mixture to a piping bag fitted with a large plain nozzle. As soon as the water is boiling, pipe 10–12 short lengths of the mixture into the water, using a sharp knife to cut the gnocchi as you go.

Bring the water back to the boil and cook the gnocchi for 3–4 minutes, or until they begin to rise to the surface. Remove with a slotted spoon, drain on absorbent kitchen paper and transfer to a warmed serving dish. Cook the gnocchi in batches if necessary.

Melt the butter in a small frying pan and when foaming add the garlic and remaining basil. Remove from the heat and immediately pour over the cooked gnocchi. Season well with salt and pepper and serve immediately with extra grated Parmesan cheese.

Try This: FOR AN ALTERNATIVE: 132   FOR A MORE SUBSTANTIAL OPTION: 188

Tagliatelle with Brown Butter, Asparagus & Parmesan

SERVES 6

fresh pasta (*see* Fresh
  Tagliatelle with Courgettes,
  page 126) or 450 g/1 lb
  dried tagliatelle, such as
  the white and green variety
350 g/12 oz asparagus,
  trimmed and cut into
  short lengths

75 g/3 oz unsalted butter
1 garlic clove, peeled
  and sliced
25 g/1 oz flaked hazelnuts
  or whole hazelnuts,
  roughly chopped
1 tbsp freshly chopped parsley
1 tbsp freshly snipped chives

salt and freshly ground
  black pepper
50 g/2 oz freshly grated
  Parmesan cheese,
  to serve

If using fresh pasta, prepare the dough according to the recipe on page 126. Cut into tagliatelle, wind into nests and reserve on a floured tea towel until ready to cook.

Bring a pan of lightly salted water to the boil. Add the asparagus and cook for 1 minute. Drain immediately, refresh under cold running water and drain again. Pat dry and reserve.

Melt the butter in a large frying pan, then add the garlic and hazelnuts and cook over a medium heat until the butter turns golden. Immediately remove from the heat and add the parsley, chives and asparagus. Leave for 2–3 minutes, until the asparagus is heated through.

Meanwhile, bring a large pan of lightly salted water to a rolling boil, then add the pasta nests. Cook until 'al dente': 2–3 minutes for fresh pasta and according to the packet instructions for dried pasta. Drain the pasta thoroughly and return to the pan. Add the asparagus mixture and toss together. Season to taste with salt and pepper and tip into a warmed serving dish. Serve immediately with grated Parmesan cheese.

Try This: FOR AN ALTERNATIVE: 126   FOR A MORE SUBSTANTIAL OPTION: 270

Tiny Pasta with Fresh Herb Sauce

SERVES 6

375 g/13 oz tripolini (small bows with rounded ends) or small farfalle
2 tbsp freshly chopped flat-leaf parsley
2 tbsp freshly chopped basil
1 tbsp freshly snipped chives
1 tbsp freshly chopped chervil
1 tbsp freshly chopped tarragon
1 tbsp freshly chopped sage
1 tbsp freshly chopped oregano
1 tbsp freshly chopped marjoram
1 tbsp freshly chopped thyme
1 tbsp freshly chopped rosemary
finely grated zest of 1 lemon
75 ml/3 fl oz extra virgin olive oil
2 garlic cloves, peeled and finely chopped
½ tsp dried chilli flakes
salt and freshly ground black pepper
freshly grated Parmesan cheese, to serve

Bring a large pan of lightly salted water to a rolling boil. Add the pasta and cook according to the packet instructions, or until 'al dente'.

Meanwhile, place all the herbs, the lemon zest, olive oil, garlic and chilli flakes in a heavy-based pan. Heat gently for 2–3 minutes, or until the herbs turn bright green and become very fragrant. Remove from the heat and season to taste with salt and pepper.

Drain the pasta thoroughly, reserving 2–3 tablespoons of the cooking water. Transfer the pasta to a large warmed bowl.

Pour the heated herb mixture over the pasta and toss together until thoroughly mixed. Check and adjust the seasoning, adding a little of the pasta cooking water if the pasta mixture seems a bit dry. Transfer to warmed serving dishes and serve immediately with grated Parmesan cheese.

Try This: FOR AN ALTERNATIVE: 144   FOR A MORE SUBSTANTIAL OPTION: 266

Tagliarini with Broad Beans, Saffron & Crème Fraîche

SERVES 2–3

225 g/8 oz fresh young broad beans in pods or 100 g/3½ oz frozen broad beans, thawed
1 tbsp olive oil
1 garlic clove, peeled

and chopped
small handful basil leaves, shredded
200 ml/7 fl oz crème fraîche
large pinch saffron strands
350 g/12 oz tagliarini

salt and freshly ground black pepper
1 tbsp freshly snipped chives
freshly grated Parmesan cheese, to serve

If using fresh broad beans, bring a pan of lightly salted water to the boil. Pod the beans and drop them into the boiling water for 1 minute. Drain and refresh under cold water. Drain again. Remove the outer skin of the beans and discard. If using thawed frozen broad beans, remove and discard the skins. Reserve the peeled beans.

Heat the olive oil in a saucepan. Add the peeled broad beans and the garlic and cook gently for 2–3 minutes. Stir in the basil, the crème fraîche and the pinch of saffron strands and simmer for 1 minute.

Meanwhile, bring a large pan of lightly salted water to a rolling boil. Add the pasta and cook according to the packet instructions, or until 'al dente'. Drain the pasta well and add to the sauce. Toss together and season to taste with salt and pepper.

Transfer the pasta and sauce to a warmed serving dish. Sprinkle with snipped chives and serve immediately with Parmesan cheese.

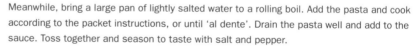

Try This: FOR AN ALTERNATIVE: 108   FOR A MORE SUBSTANTIAL OPTION: 276

Pasta with Walnut Sauce

SERVES 4

50 g/2 oz walnuts, toasted
3 spring onions, trimmed
  and chopped
2 garlic cloves, peeled
  and sliced

1 tbsp freshly chopped
  parsley or basil
5 tbsp extra virgin olive oil
salt and freshly ground
  black pepper

450 g/1 lb broccoli,
  cut into florets
350 g/12 oz pasta shapes
1 red chilli, deseeded and
  finely chopped

Place the toasted walnuts in a blender or food processor with the chopped spring onions, one of the garlic cloves and parsley or basil. Blend to a fairly smooth paste, then gradually add 3 tablespoons of the olive oil, until it is well mixed into the paste. Season the walnut paste to taste with salt and pepper and reserve.

Bring a large pan of lightly salted water to a rolling boil. Add the broccoli, return to the boil and cook for 2 minutes. Remove the broccoli, using a slotted draining spoon and refresh under cold running water. Drain again and pat dry on absorbent kitchen paper.

Bring the water back to a rolling boil. Add the pasta and cook according to the packet instructions, or until 'al dente'.

Meanwhile, heat the remaining oil in a frying pan. Add the remaining garlic and chilli. Cook gently for 2 minutes, or until softened. Add the broccoli and walnut paste. Cook for a further 3–4 minutes, or until heated through.

Drain the pasta thoroughly and transfer to a large warmed serving bowl. Pour over the walnut and broccoli sauce. Toss together, adjust the seasoning and serve immediately.

Try This: FOR AN ALTERNATIVE: 114   FOR A MORE SUBSTANTIAL OPTION: 270

Hot Herby Mushrooms

SERVES 4

4 thin slices of white bread,
  crusts removed
125 g/4 oz chestnut
  mushrooms, wiped
  and sliced
125 g/4 oz oyster

mushrooms, wiped
1 garlic clove, peeled
  and crushed
1 tsp Dijon mustard
300 ml/½ pint chicken stock
salt and freshly ground

black pepper
1 tbsp freshly chopped
  parsley
1 tbsp freshly snipped chives,
  plus extra to garnish
mixed salad leaves, to serve

Preheat the oven to 180°C/350°F/Gas Mark 4. With a rolling pin, roll each piece of bread out as thinly as possible. Press each piece of bread into a 10 cm/4 inch tartlet tin. Push each piece firmly down, then bake in the preheated oven for 20 minutes.

Place the mushrooms in a frying pan with the garlic, mustard and chicken stock and stir-fry over a moderate heat until the mushrooms are tender and the liquid is reduced by half.

Carefully remove the mushrooms from the frying pan with a slotted spoon and transfer to a heat-resistant dish. Cover with tinfoil and place in the bottom of the oven to keep the mushrooms warm.

Boil the remaining pan juices until reduced to a thick sauce. Season with salt and pepper. Stir the parsley and the chives into the mushroom mixture.

Place one bread tartlet case on each plate and divide the mushroom mixture between them. Spoon over the pan juices, garnish with the chives and serve immediately with mixed salad leaves.

Try This: FOR AN ALTERNATIVE: 146   FOR A MORE SUBSTANTIAL OPTION: 266

Wild Mushroom & Garlic Galettes

SERVES 6

1 quantity quick flaky pastry, chilled
1 onion, peeled
1 red chilli, deseeded
2 garlic cloves, peeled
275 g/10 oz mixed

mushrooms e.g. oyster, chestnuts, morels, ceps and chanterelles
25 g/1 oz butter
2 tbsp freshly chopped parsley

125 g/4 oz mozzarella cheese, sliced

To serve:
cherry tomatoes
mixed green salad leaves

Preheat the oven to 220°C/425°F/Gas Mark 7. On a lightly floured surface roll out the chilled pastry very thinly. Cut out 6 x 15 cm/6 inch circles and place on a lightly oiled baking sheet.

Thinly slice the onion, then divide into rings and reserve. Thinly slice the chilli and slice the garlic into wafer-thin slivers. Add to the onions and reserve.

Wipe or lightly rinse the mushrooms. Halve or quarter any large mushrooms and keep the small ones whole.

Heat the butter in a frying pan and sauté the onion, chilli and garlic gently for about 3 minutes. Add the mushrooms and cook for about 5 minutes, or until beginning to soften. Stir the parsley into the mushroom mixture and drain off any excess liquid.

Pile the mushroom mixture on to the pastry circles within 5 mm/¼ inches of the edge. Arrange the sliced mozzarella cheese on top.

Bake in the preheated oven for 12–15 minutes, or until golden brown, and serve with the tomatoes and salad.

Try This: FOR AN ALTERNATIVE: 148 FOR A MORE SUBSTANTIAL OPTION: 210

Fennel & Caramelised Shallot Tartlets

SERVES 6

For the cheese pastry:
176 g/6 oz plain white flour
75 g/3 oz slightly salted butter
50 g/2 oz Gruyère cheese,
    grated
1 small egg yolk

For the filling:
2 tbsp olive oil
225 g/8 oz shallots,
    peeled and halved
1 fennel bulb, trimmed
    and sliced
1 tsp soft brown sugar
1 medium egg

150 ml/¼ pint double cream
salt and freshly ground
    black pepper
25 g/1 oz Gruyère cheese,
    grated
½ tsp ground cinnamon
mixed salad leaves, to serve

Preheat the oven to 200°C/400°F/Gas Mark 6. Sift the flour into a bowl, then rub in the butter, using the fingertips. Stir in the cheese, then add the egg yolk with about 2 tablespoons of cold water. Mix to a firm dough, then knead lightly. Wrap in clingfilm and chill in the refrigerator for 30 minutes.

Roll out the pastry on a lightly floured surface and use to line 6 x 10 cm/4 inch individual flan tins or patty tins which are about 2 cm/¾ inch deep.

Line the pastry cases with greaseproof paper and fill with baking beans or rice. Bake blind in the preheated oven for about 10 minutes, then remove the paper and beans.

Heat the oil in a frying pan, add the shallots and fennel and fry gently for 5 minutes. Sprinkle with the sugar and cook for a further 10 minutes, stirring occasionally until lightly caramelised. Reserve until cooled.

Beat together the egg and cream and season to taste with salt and pepper. Divide the shallot mixture between the pastry cases. Pour over the egg mixture and sprinkle with the cheese and cinnamon. Bake for 20 minutes, until golden and set. Serve with the salad leaves.

Try This: FOR AN ALTERNATIVE: 72   FOR A MORE SUBSTANTIAL OPTION: 194

Ginger & Garlic Potatoes

SERVES 4

700 g/1½ lb potatoes
2.5 cm/1 inch piece of root
   ginger, peeled and
   coarsely chopped
3 garlic cloves, peeled
   and chopped
½ tsp turmeric

1 tsp salt
½ tsp cayenne pepper
5 tbsp vegetable oil
1 tsp whole fennel seeds
1 large eating apple, cored
   and diced
6 spring onions, trimmed

and sliced diagonally
1 tbsp freshly
   chopped coriander

To serve:
assorted bitter salad leaves
curry-flavoured mayonnaise

Scrub the potatoes, then place, unpeeled, in a large saucepan and cover with boiling salted water. Bring to the boil and cook for 15 minutes, then drain and leave the potatoes to cool completely. Peel and cut into 2.5 cm/1 inch cubes.

Place the root ginger, garlic, turmeric, salt and cayenne pepper in a food processor and blend for 1 minute. With the motor still running, slowly add 3 tablespoons of water and blend into a paste. Alternatively, pound the ingredients to a paste with a pestle and mortar.

Heat the oil in a large heavy-based frying pan and when hot, but not smoking, add the fennel seeds and fry for a few minutes. Stir in the ginger paste and cook for 2 minutes, stirring frequently. Take care not to burn the mixture.

Reduce the heat, then add the potatoes and cook for 5–7 minutes, stirring frequently, until the potatoes have a golden-brown crust. Add the diced apple and spring onions, then sprinkle with the freshly chopped coriander. Heat through for 2 minutes, then serve on assorted salad leaves with curry-flavoured mayonnaise.

Try This: FOR AN ALTERNATIVE: 184   FOR A MORE SUBSTANTIAL OPTION: 206

Potato Pancakes

SERVES 6

For the sauce:
4 tbsp crème fraîche
1 tbsp horseradish sauce
grated rind and juice
 of 1 lime
1 tbsp freshly
 snipped chives

For the pancakes:
225 g/8 oz floury potatoes,
 peeled and cut into chunks
1 small egg white
2 tbsp milk
2 tsp self-raising flour
1 tbsp freshly chopped thyme

large pinch of salt
a little vegetable oil,
 for frying
225 g/8 oz smoked mackerel
 fillets, skinned and
 roughly chopped
fresh herbs, to garnish

To make the sauce, mix together the crème fraîche, horseradish sauce, lime rind and juice and chives. Cover and reserve.

Place the potatoes in a large saucepan and cover with lightly salted boiling water. Bring back to the boil, cover and simmer for 15 minutes, or until the potatoes are tender. Drain and mash until smooth. Cool for 5 minutes, then whisk in the egg white, milk, flour, thyme and salt to form a thick smooth batter. Leave to stand for 30 minutes, then stir before using.

Heat a little oil in a heavy-based frying pan. Add 2–3 large spoonfuls of batter to make a small pancake and cook for 1–2 minutes until golden. Flip the pancake and cook for a further minute, or until golden. Repeat with the remaining batter to make 8 pancakes.

Arrange the pancakes on a plate and top with the smoked mackerel. Garnish with herbs and serve immediately with spoonfuls of the sauce.

Try This: FOR AN ALTERNATIVE: 196   FOR A MORE SUBSTANTIAL OPTION: 230

Soups

Vietnamese Beef & Rice Noodle Soup

SERVES 4–6

For the beef stock:
900 g/2 lb meaty beef bones
1 large onion, peeled and
quartered
2 carrots, peeled and
cut into chunks
2 celery stalks, trimmed
and sliced
1 leek, washed and sliced
into chunks

2 garlic cloves, unpeeled
and lightly crushed
3 whole star anise
1 tsp black peppercorns

For the soup:
175 g/6 oz dried rice
stick noodles
4–6 spring onions, trimmed
and diagonally sliced

1 red chilli, deseeded and
diagonally sliced
1 small bunch fresh coriander
1 small bunch fresh mint
350 g/12 oz fillet steak,
very thinly sliced
salt and freshly ground
black pepper

Place all the ingredients for the beef stock into a large stock pot or saucepan and cover with cold water. Bring to the boil and skim off any scum that rises to the surface. Reduce the heat and simmer gently, partially covered, for 2–3 hours, skimming occasionally. Strain into a large bowl and leave to cool, then skim off the fat. Chill in the refrigerator and when cold remove any fat from the surface. Pour 1.7 litres/3 pints of the stock into a large wok and reserve.

Cover the noodles with warm water and leave for 3 minutes, or until just softened. Drain, then cut into 10 cm/4 inch lengths.

Arrange the spring onions and chilli on a serving platter or large plate. Strip the leaves from the coriander and mint and arrange them in piles on the plate.

Bring the stock in the wok to the boil over a high heat. Add the noodles and simmer for about 2 minutes, or until tender. Add the beef strips and simmer for about 1 minute. Season to taste with salt and pepper. Ladle the soup with the noodles and beef strips into individual soup bowls and serve immediately with the plate of condiments handed around separately.

Try This: FOR AN ALTERNATIVE: 170 FOR A MORE SUBSTANTIAL OPTION: 200

Bacon & Split Pea Soup

SERVES 4

50 g/2 oz dried split peas
25 g/1 oz butter
1 garlic clove, peeled and
  finely chopped
1 medium onion, peeled and
  thinly sliced
175 g/6 oz long-grain rice

2 tbsp tomato purée
1.1 litres/2 pints vegetable
  or chicken stock
175 g/6 oz carrots, peeled
  and finely diced
125 g/4 oz streaky bacon,
  finely chopped

salt and freshly ground
  black pepper
2 tbsp freshly
  chopped parsley
4 tbsp single cream
warm crusty garlic bread,
  to serve

Cover the dried split peas with plenty of cold water, cover loosely and leave to soak for a minimum of 12 hours, preferably overnight.

Melt the butter in a heavy-based saucepan, add the garlic and onion and cook for 2–3 minutes, without colouring. Add the rice, drained split peas and tomato purée and cook for 2–3 minutes, stirring constantly to prevent sticking. Add the stock, bring to the boil, then reduce the heat and simmer for 20–25 minutes, or until the rice and peas are tender. Remove from the heat and leave to cool.

Blend about three-quarters of the soup in a food processor or blender to form a smooth purée. Pour the purée into the remaining soup in the saucepan. Add the carrots to the saucepan and cook for a further 10–12 minutes, or until the carrots are tender.

Meanwhile, place the bacon in a non-stick frying pan and cook over a gentle heat until the bacon is crisp. Remove and drain on absorbent kitchen paper.

Season the soup with salt and pepper to taste, then stir in the parsley and cream. Reheat for 2–3 minutes, then ladle into soup bowls. Sprinkle with the bacon and serve immediately with warm garlic bread.

Try This: FOR AN ALTERNATIVE: 160 FOR A MORE SUBSTANTIAL OPTION: 202

White Bean Soup with Parmesan Croûtons

SERVES 4

3 thick slices of white bread, cut into 1 cm/½ inch cubes
3 tbsp groundnut oil
2 tbsp Parmesan cheese, finely grated
1 tbsp light olive oil
1 large onion, peeled and finely chopped

50 g/2 oz unsmoked bacon lardons (or thick slices of bacon, diced)
1 tbsp fresh thyme leaves
2 x 400 g cans cannellini beans, drained
900 ml/1½ pints chicken stock

salt and freshly ground black pepper
1 tbsp prepared pesto sauce
50 g/2 oz piece of pepperoni sausage, diced
1 tbsp fresh lemon juice
1 tbsp fresh basil, roughly shredded

Preheat oven to 200°C/400°F/Gas Mark 6. Place the cubes of bread in a bowl and pour over the groundnut oil. Stir to coat the bread, then sprinkle over the Parmesan cheese. Place on a lightly oiled baking tray and bake in the preheated oven for 10 minutes, or until crisp and golden.

Heat the olive oil in a large saucepan and cook the onion for 4–5 minutes until softened. Add the bacon and thyme and cook for a further 3 minutes. Stir in the beans, stock and black pepper and simmer gently for 5 minutes.

Place half the bean mixture and liquid into a food processor and blend until smooth.

Return the purée to the saucepan. Stir in the pesto sauce, pepperoni sausage and lemon juice and season to taste with salt and pepper.

Return the soup to the heat and cook for a further 2–3 minutes, or until piping hot. Place some of the beans in each serving bowl and add a ladleful of soup. Garnish with shredded basil and serve immediately with the croûtons scattered over the top.

Try This: FOR AN ALTERNATIVE: 158   FOR A MORE SUBSTANTIAL OPTION: 262

Classic Minestrone

SERVES 6–8

25 g/1 oz butter
3 tbsp olive oil
3 rashers streaky bacon
1 large onion, peeled
1 garlic clove, peeled
1 celery stick, trimmed
2 carrots, peeled

400 g can chopped tomatoes
1.1 litre/2 pints chicken stock
175 g/6 oz green cabbage,
   finely shredded
50 g/2 oz French beans,
   trimmed and halved
3 tbsp frozen petits pois

50 g/2 oz spaghetti, broken
   into short pieces
salt and freshly ground
   black pepper
Parmesan cheese shavings,
   to garnish
crusty bread, to serve

Heat the butter and olive oil together in a large saucepan. Chop the bacon and add to the saucepan. Cook for 3–4 minutes, then remove with a slotted spoon and reserve.

Finely chop the onion, garlic, celery and carrots and add to the saucepan, one ingredient at a time, stirring well after each addition. Cover and cook gently for 8–10 minutes, until the vegetables are softened.

Add the chopped tomatoes, with their juice and the stock, bring to the boil then cover the saucepan with a lid, reduce the heat and simmer gently for about 20 minutes.

Stir in the cabbage, beans, peas and spaghetti pieces. Cover and simmer for a further 20 minutes, or until all the ingredients are tender. Season to taste with salt and pepper.

Return the cooked bacon to the saucepan and bring the soup to the boil. Serve the soup immediately with Parmesan cheese shavings sprinkled on the top and plenty of crusty bread to accompany it.

Try This: FOR AN ALTERNATIVE: 164   FOR A MORE SUBSTANTIAL OPTION: 210

Pasta & Bean Soup

SERVES 4–6

3 tbsp olive oil
2 celery sticks, trimmed and
  finely chopped
100 g/3½ oz prosciutto
  or prosciutto di speck,
  cut in pieces
1 red chilli, deseeded and
  finely chopped
2 large potatoes, peeled and
  cut into 2.5 cm/1 in cubes
2 garlic cloves, peeled and
  finely chopped
3 ripe plum tomatoes,
  skinned and chopped
1 x 400 g cans borlotti
  beans, drained and rinsed
1 litre/1¾ pints chicken or
  vegetable stock
100 g/3½ oz pasta shapes
large handful basil leaves,
  torn
salt and freshly ground
  black pepper
shredded basil leaves,
  to garnish
crusty bread, to serve

Heat the olive oil in a heavy-based pan, add the celery and prosciutto and cook gently for 6–8 minutes, or until softened. Add the chopped chilli and potato cubes and cook for a further 10 minutes.

Add the garlic to the chilli and potato mixture and cook for 1 minute. Add the chopped tomatoes and simmer for 5 minutes. Stir in two-thirds of the beans, then pour in the chicken or vegetable stock and bring to the boil.

Add the pasta shapes to the soup stock and return it to simmering point. Cook the pasta for about 10 minutes, or until 'al dente'.

Meanwhile, place the remaining beans in a food processor or blender and blend with enough of the soup stock to make a smooth, thinnish purée.

When the pasta is cooked, stir in the puréed beans with the torn basil. Season the soup to taste with salt and pepper. Ladle into serving bowls, garnish with shredded basil and serve immediately with plenty of crusty bread.

Try This: FOR AN ALTERNATIVE: 160 FOR A MORE SUBSTANTIAL OPTION: 262

Rice Soup with Potato Sticks

SERVES 4

175 g/6 oz butter
1 tsp olive oil
1 large onion, peeled
and finely chopped
4 slices Parma ham,
chopped
100 g/3½ oz Arborio rice

1.1 litres/2 pints
chicken stock
350 g/12 oz frozen peas
salt and freshly ground black
pepper
1 medium egg
125 g/4 oz self-raising flour

175 g/6 oz mashed potato
1 tbsp milk
1 tbsp poppy seeds
1 tbsp Parmesan cheese,
finely grated
1 tbsp freshly chopped
parsley

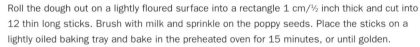

Preheat oven to 190°C/375°F/Gas Mark 5. Heat 25 g/1 oz of the butter and the olive oil in a saucepan and cook the onion for 4–5 minutes until softened, then add the Parma ham and cook for about 1 minute. Stir in the rice, the stock and the peas. Season to taste with salt and pepper and simmer for 10–15 minutes, or until the rice is tender.

Beat the egg and 125 g/4 oz of the butter together until smooth, then beat in the flour, a pinch of salt and the potato. Work the ingredients together to form a soft, pliable dough, adding a little more flour if necessary.

Roll the dough out on a lightly floured surface into a rectangle 1 cm/½ inch thick and cut into 12 thin long sticks. Brush with milk and sprinkle on the poppy seeds. Place the sticks on a lightly oiled baking tray and bake in the preheated oven for 15 minutes, or until golden.

When the rice is cooked, stir the remaining butter and Parmesan cheese into the soup and sprinkle the chopped parsley over the top. Serve immediately with the warm potato sticks.

Try This: FOR AN ALTERNATIVE: 178   FOR A MORE SUBSTANTIAL OPTION: 206

Creamy Caribbean Chicken & Coconut Soup

SERVES 4

6–8 spring onions
2 garlic cloves
1 red chilli
175 g/6 oz cooked chicken, shredded or diced
2 tbsp vegetable oil
1 tsp ground turmeric

300 ml/½ pint coconut milk
900 ml/1½ pints chicken stock
50 g/2 oz small soup pasta or spaghetti, broken into small pieces
½ lemon, sliced
salt and freshly ground

black pepper
1–2 tbsp freshly chopped coriander
sprigs of fresh coriander, to garnish

Trim the spring onions and thinly slice; peel the garlic and finely chop. Cut off the top from the chilli, slit down the side and remove seeds and membrane, then finely chop and reserve.

Remove and discard any skin or bones from the cooked chicken and shred using 2 forks and reserve.

Heat a large wok, add the oil and when hot add the spring onions, garlic and chilli and stir-fry for 2 minutes, or until the onion has softened. Stir in the turmeric and cook for 1 minute.

Blend the coconut milk with the chicken stock until smooth, then pour into the wok. Add the pasta or spaghetti with the lemon slices and bring to the boil. Simmer, half-covered, for 10–12 minutes, or until the pasta is tender; stir occasionally.

Remove the lemon slices from the wok and add the chicken. Season to taste with salt and pepper and simmer for 2–3 minutes, or until the chicken is heated through thoroughly.

Stir in the chopped coriander and ladle into heated bowls. Garnish with sprigs of fresh coriander and serve immediately.

Try This: FOR AN ALTERNATIVE: 186   FOR A MORE SUBSTANTIAL OPTION: 214

Laksa Malayan Rice Noodle Soup

SERVES 4–6

1.1 kg/2½ lb corn-fed, free-range chicken
1 tsp black peppercorns
1 tbsp vegetable oil
1 large onion, peeled and thinly sliced
2 garlic cloves, peeled and finely chopped
2.5 cm/1 inch piece fresh root ginger, peeled and thinly sliced
1 tsp ground coriander
2 red chillies, deseeded and diagonally sliced
1–2 tsp hot curry paste
400 ml/14 fl oz coconut milk
450 g/1 lb large raw prawns, peeled and deveined
½ small head of Chinese leaves, thinly shredded
1 tsp sugar
2 spring onions, trimmed and thinly sliced
125 g/4 oz beansprouts
250 g/9 oz rice noodles or rice sticks, soaked as per packet instructions
fresh mint leaves, to garnish

Put the chicken in a large saucepan with the peppercorns and cover with cold water. Bring to the boil, skimming off any scum that rises to the surface. Simmer, partially covered, for about 1 hour. Remove the chicken and cool. Skim any fat from the stock and strain through a muslin-lined sieve and reserve. Remove the meat from the carcass, shred and reserve.

Heat a large wok, add the oil and when hot, add the onions and stir-fry for 2 minutes, or until they begin to colour. Stir in the garlic, ginger, coriander, chillies and curry paste and stir-fry for a further 2 minutes. Carefully pour in the reserved stock (you need at least 1.1 litres/2 pints) and simmer gently, partially covered, for 10 minutes, or until slightly reduced.

Add the coconut milk, prawns, Chinese leaves, sugar, spring onions and beansprouts and simmer for 3 minutes, stirring occasionally. Add the reserved shredded chicken, and cook for a further 2 minutes. Drain the noodles and divide between 4–6 soup bowls. Ladle the hot stock and vegetables over the noodles, making sure each serving has some prawns and chicken. Garnish each bowl with fresh mint leaves and serve immediately.

Try This: FOR AN ALTERNATIVE: 156   FOR A MORE SUBSTANTIAL OPTION: 224

Thai Hot-&-Sour Prawn Soup

SERVES 6

700 g/1½ lb large
  raw prawns
2 tbsp vegetable oil
3–4 stalks lemon grass,
  outer leaves discarded
  and coarsely chopped
2.5 cm/1 inch piece fresh
  root ginger, peeled and
  finely chopped
2–3 garlic cloves, peeled

and crushed
small bunch fresh coriander,
  leaves stripped and
  reserved, stems
  finely chopped
½ tsp freshly ground
  black pepper
1.8 litres/3¼ pints water
1–2 small red chillies,
  deseeded and thinly sliced

1–2 small green chillies,
  deseeded and thinly sliced
6 kaffir lime leaves, thinly
  shredded
4 spring onions, trimmed
  and diagonally sliced
1–2 tbsp Thai fish sauce
1–2 tbsp freshly squeezed
  lime juice

Remove the heads from the prawns by twisting away from the body and reserve. Peel the prawns, leaving the tails on and reserve the shells with the heads. Using a sharp knife, remove the black vein from the back of the prawns. Rinse and dry the prawns and reserve. Rinse and dry the heads and shells.

Heat a wok, add the oil and, when hot, add the prawn heads and shells, the lemon grass, ginger, garlic, coriander stems and black pepper and stir-fry for 2–3 minutes, or until the prawn heads and shells turn pink and all the ingredients are coloured.

Carefully add the water to the wok and return to the boil, skimming off any scum which rises to the surface. Simmer over a medium heat for 10 minutes or until slightly reduced. Strain through a fine sieve and return the clear prawn stock to the wok.

Bring the stock back to the boil and add the reserved prawns, chillies, lime leaves and spring onions and simmer for 3 minutes, or until the prawns turn pink. Season with the fish sauce and lime juice. Spoon into heated soup bowls, dividing the prawns evenly and float a few coriander leaves over the surface.

Try This: FOR AN ALTERNATIVE: 170   FOR A MORE SUBSTANTIAL OPTION: 226

Tuna Chowder

SERVES 4

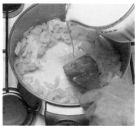

2 tsp oil
1 onion, peeled and
    finely chopped
2 sticks of celery, trimmed
    and finely sliced
1 tbsp plain flour

600 ml/1 pint skimmed milk
200 g can tuna in water
320 g can sweetcorn in
    water, drained
2 tsp freshly chopped thyme
salt and freshly ground

black pepper
pinch cayenne pepper
2 tbsp freshly
    chopped parsley

Heat the oil in a large heavy-based saucepan. Add the onion and celery and gently cook for about 5 minutes, stirring from time to time until the onion is softened. Stir in the flour and cook for about 1 minute to thicken.

Draw the pan off the heat and gradually pour in the milk, stirring throughout.

Add the tuna and its liquid, the drained sweetcorn and the thyme. Mix gently, then bring to the boil. Cover and simmer for 5 minutes. Remove the pan from the heat and season to taste with salt and pepper.

Sprinkle the chowder with the cayenne pepper and chopped parsley. Divide into soup bowls and serve immediately.

Try This: FOR AN ALTERNATIVE: 176 FOR A MORE SUBSTANTIAL OPTION: 232

Pumpkin & Smoked Haddock Soup

SERVES 4-6

2 tbsp olive oil
1 medium onion,
    peeled and chopped
2 garlic cloves,
    peeled and chopped
3 celery stalks,
    trimmed and chopped

700 g/1½ lb pumpkin,
    peeled, deseeded and
    cut into chunks
450 g/1 lb potatoes, peeled
    and cut into chunks
750 ml/1¼ pints chicken
    stock, heated

125 ml/4 fl oz dry sherry
200 g/7 oz smoked
    haddock fillet
150 ml/¼ pint milk
freshly ground black pepper
2 tbsp freshly
    chopped parsley

Heat the oil in a large heavy-based saucepan and gently cook the onion, garlic, and celery for about 10 minutes. This will release the sweetness but not colour the vegetables. Add the pumpkin and potatoes to the saucepan and stir to coat the vegetables with the oil.

Gradually pour in the stock and bring to the boil. Cover, then reduce the heat and simmer for 25 minutes, stirring occasionally. Stir in the dry sherry, then remove the saucepan from the heat and leave to cool for 5–10 minutes.

Blend the mixture in a food processor or blender to form a chunky purée and return to the cleaned saucepan.

Meanwhile, place the fish in a shallow frying pan. Pour in the milk with 3 tablespoons of water and bring to almost boiling point. Reduce the heat, cover and simmer for 6 minutes, or until the fish is cooked and flakes easily. Remove from the heat and, using a slotted spoon, remove the fish from the liquid, reserving both liquid and fish.

Discard the skin and any bones from the fish and flake into pieces. Stir the fish liquid into the soup, together with the flaked fish. Season with freshly ground black pepper, stir in the parsley and serve immediately.

Try This: FOR AN ALTERNATIVE: 186   FOR A MORE SUBSTANTIAL OPTION: 272

Rice & Tomato Soup

SERVES 4

150 g/5 oz easy-cook
  basmati rice
400 g can chopped tomatoes
2 garlic cloves, peeled
  and crushed
grated rind of ½ lime

2 tbsp extra-virgin olive oil
1 tsp sugar
salt and freshly ground
  pepper
300 ml/½ pint vegetable
  stock or water

For the croûtons:
2 tbsp prepared pesto sauce
2 tbsp olive oil
6 thin slices ciabatta bread,
  cut into 1 cm/½ inch cubes

Preheat the oven to 220°C/425°F/Gas Mark 7. Rinse and drain the basmati rice. Place the canned tomatoes with their juice in a large heavy-based saucepan with the garlic, lime rind, oil and sugar. Season to taste with salt and pepper. Bring to the boil, then reduce the heat, cover and simmer for 10 minutes.

Add the boiling vegetable stock or water and the rice, then cook, uncovered, for a further 15–20 minutes, or until the rice is tender. If the soup is too thick, add a little more water. Reserve and keep warm, if the croûtons are not ready.

Meanwhile, to make the croûtons, mix the pesto and olive oil in a large bowl. Add the bread cubes and toss until they are coated completely with the mixture. Spread on a baking sheet and bake in the preheated oven for 10–15 minutes, until golden and crisp, turning them over halfway through cooking. Serve the soup immediately sprinkled with the warm croûtons.

Try This: FOR AN ALTERNATIVE: 180 FOR A MORE SUBSTANTIAL OPTION: 208

Rich Tomato Soup with Roasted Red Peppers

SERVES 4

2 tsp light olive oil
700 g/1½ lb red peppers,
   halved and deseeded
450 g/1 lb ripe plum
   tomatoes, halved

2 onions, unpeeled and
   quartered
4 garlic cloves, unpeeled
600 ml/1 pint chicken stock
salt and freshly ground

black pepper
4 tbsp soured cream
1 tbsp freshly
   shredded basil

Preheat oven to 200°C/400°F/Gas Mark 6. Lightly oil a roasting tin with 1 teaspoon of the olive oil. Place the peppers and tomatoes cut side down in the roasting tin with the onion quarters and the garlic cloves. Spoon over the remaining oil.

Bake in the preheated oven for 30 minutes, or until the skins on the peppers have started to blacken and blister. Allow the vegetables to cool for about 10 minutes, then remove the skins, stalks and seeds from the peppers. Peel away the skins from the tomatoes and onions and squeeze out the garlic.

Place the cooked vegetables into a blender or food processor and blend until smooth. Add the stock and blend again to form a smooth purée. Pour the puréed soup through a sieve, if a smooth soup is preferred, then pour into a saucepan. Bring to the boil, simmer gently for 2–3 minutes, and season to taste with salt and pepper. Serve hot with a swirl of soured cream and a sprinkling of shredded basil on the top.

Try This: FOR AN ALTERNATIVE: 182 FOR A MORE SUBSTANTIAL OPTION: 260

Tomato & Basil Soup

SERVES 4

1.1 kg/2½ lb ripe
   tomatoes, cut in half
2 garlic cloves
1 tsp olive oil
1 tbsp balsamic vinegar

1 tbsp dark brown sugar
1 tbsp tomato purée
300 ml/½ pint
   vegetable stock
6 tbsp low-fat natural yogurt

2 tbsp freshly chopped basil
salt and freshly ground
   black pepper
small basil leaves,
   to garnish

Preheat the oven to 200°C/400°F/Gas Mark 6. Evenly spread the tomatoes and unpeeled garlic in a single layer in a large roasting tin.

Mix the oil and vinegar together. Drizzle over the tomatoes and sprinkle with the dark brown sugar. Roast the tomatoes in the preheated oven for 20 minutes until tender and lightly charred in places.

Remove from the oven and allow to cool slightly. When cool enough to handle, squeeze the softened flesh of the garlic from the papery skin. Place with the charred tomatoes in a nylon sieve over a saucepan.

Press the garlic and tomato through the sieve with the back of a wooden spoon. When all the flesh has been sieved, add the tomato purée and vegetable stock to the pan. Heat gently, stirring occasionally.

In a small bowl beat the yogurt and basil together and season to taste with salt and pepper. Stir the basil yogurt into the soup. Garnish with basil leaves and serve immediately.

Try This: FOR AN ALTERNATIVE: 180   FOR A MORE SUBSTANTIAL OPTION: 268

Rocket & Potato Soup
with Garlic Croûtons

SERVES 4

700 g/1½ lb baby
  new potatoes
1.1 litres/2 pints chicken
  or vegetable stock
50 g/2 oz rocket leaves
125 g/4 oz thick white
  sliced bread

50 g/2 oz unsalted butter
1 tsp groundnut oil
2–4 garlic cloves, peeled and
  chopped
125 g/4 oz stale ciabatta
  bread, with the crusts
  removed

4 tbsp olive oil
salt and freshly ground
  black pepper
2 tbsp Parmesan cheese,
  finely grated

Place the potatoes in a large saucepan, cover with the stock and simmer gently for 10 minutes. Add the rocket leaves and simmer for a further 5–10 minutes, or until the potatoes are soft and the rocket has wilted.

Meanwhile, make the croûtons. Cut the thick, white sliced bread into small cubes and reserve. Heat the butter and groundnut oil in a small frying pan and cook the garlic for 1 minute, stirring well. Remove the garlic. Add the bread cubes to the butter and oil mixture in the frying pan and sauté, stirring continuously, until they are golden brown. Drain the croûtons on absorbent kitchen paper and reserve.

Cut the ciabatta bread into small dice and stir into the soup. Cover the saucepan and leave to stand for 10 minutes, or until the bread has absorbed a lot of the liquid.

Stir in the olive oil, season to taste with salt and pepper and serve at once with a few of the garlic croûtons scattered over the top and a little grated Parmesan cheese.

Try This: FOR AN ALTERNATIVE: 194   FOR A MORE SUBSTANTIAL OPTION: 282

Cream of Pumpkin Soup

SERVES 6–8

900 g/2 lb pumpkin flesh
   (after peeling and
   discarding the seeds)
4 tbsp olive oil
1 large onion, peeled
1 leek, trimmed

1 carrot, peeled
2 celery sticks
4 garlic cloves,
   peeled and crushed
1.7 litres/3 pints water
salt and freshly ground

black pepper
¼ tsp freshly
   grated nutmeg
150 ml/¼ pint single cream
¼ tsp cayenne pepper
warm herby bread, to serve

Cut the skinned and de-seeded pumpkin flesh into 2.5 cm/1 inch cubes. Heat the olive oil in a large saucepan and cook the pumpkin for 2–3 minutes, coating it completely with oil. Chop the onion and leek finely and cut the carrot and celery into small dice.

Add the vegetables to the saucepan with the garlic and cook, stirring for 5 minutes, or until they have begun to soften. Cover the vegetables with the water and bring to the boil. Season with plenty of salt and pepper and the nutmeg. Cover and simmer for 15–20 minutes, or until all of the vegetables are tender.

When the vegetables are tender, remove from the heat, cool slightly then pour into a food processor or blender. Liquidise to form a smooth purée then pass through a sieve into a clean saucepan.

Adjust the seasoning to taste and add all but 2 tablespoons of the cream and enough water to obtain the correct consistency. Bring the soup to boiling point, add the cayenne pepper and serve immediately swirled with cream and warm herby bread.

Try This: FOR AN ALTERNATIVE: 188 FOR A MORE SUBSTANTIAL OPTION: 272

Cream of Spinach Soup

SERVES 6–8

1 large onion, peeled
  and chopped
5 large plump garlic cloves,
  peeled and chopped
2 medium potatoes,
  peeled and chopped
750 ml/1¼ pints cold water

1 tsp salt
450 g/1 lb spinach, washed
  and large stems removed
50 g/2 oz butter
3 tbsp flour
750 ml/1¼ pints milk
½ tsp freshly

  grated nutmeg
freshly ground black pepper
6–8 tbsp crème fraîche or
  soured cream
warm foccacia bread,
  to serve

Place the onion, garlic and potatoes in a large saucepan and cover with the cold water. Add half the salt and bring to the boil. Cover and simmer for 15–20 minutes, or until the potatoes are tender. Remove from the heat and add the spinach. Cover and set aside for 10 minutes.

Slowly melt the butter in another saucepan, add the flour and cook over a low heat for about 2 minutes. Remove the saucepan from the heat and add the milk, a little at a time, stirring continuously. Return to the heat and cook, stirring continuously, for 5–8 minutes, or until the sauce is smooth and slightly thickened. Add the freshly grated nutmeg, or to taste.

Blend the cooled potato and spinach mixture in a food processor or blender to a smooth purée, then return to the saucepan and gradually stir in the white sauce. Season to taste with salt and pepper and gently reheat, taking care not to allow the soup to boil. Ladle into soup bowls and top with spoonfuls of crème fraîche or soured cream. Serve immediately with warm foccacia bread.

Try This: FOR AN ALTERNATIVE: 184   FOR A MORE SUBSTANTIAL OPTION: 134

Carrot & Ginger Soup

SERVES 4

4 slices of bread,
    crusts removed
1 tsp yeast extract
2 tsp olive oil
1 onion, peeled and chopped
1 garlic clove,
    peeled and crushed
½ tsp ground ginger

450 g/1 lb carrots,
    peeled and chopped
1 litre/1¾ pint
    vegetable stock
2.5 cm/1 inch piece of
    root ginger, peeled
    and finely grated
salt and freshly ground

black pepper
1 tbsp lemon juice

To garnish:
chives
lemon zest

Preheat the oven to 180°C/350°F/Gas Mark 4. Roughly chop the bread. Dissolve the yeast extract in 2 tablespoons of warm water and mix with the bread.

Spread the bread cubes over a lightly oiled baking tray and bake for 20 minutes, turning half way through. Remove from the oven and reserve.

Heat the oil in a large saucepan. Gently cook the onion and garlic for 3–4 minutes. Stir in the ground ginger and cook for 1 minute to release the flavour. Add the chopped carrots, then stir in the stock and the fresh ginger. Simmer gently for 15 minutes.

Remove from the heat and allow to cool a little. Blend until smooth, then season to taste with salt and pepper. Stir in the lemon juice. Garnish with the chives and lemon zest and serve immediately.

Try This: FOR AN ALTERNATIVE: 186 FOR A MORE SUBSTANTIAL OPTION: 150

Hot–&–Sour Mushroom Soup

SERVES 4

4 tbsp sunflower oil
3 garlic cloves, peeled
   and finely chopped
3 shallots, peeled and
   finely chopped
2 large red chillies,
   deseeded and
   finely chopped
1 tbsp soft brown sugar
large pinch of salt

1 litre/1¾ pints
   vegetable stock
250 g/9 oz Thai fragrant rice
5 kaffir lime leaves, torn
2 tbsp soy sauce
grated rind and juice
   of 1 lemon
250 g/9 oz oyster
   mushrooms, wiped and
   cut into pieces

2 tbsp freshly
   chopped coriander

To garnish:
2 green chillies, deseeded
   and finely chopped
3 spring onions, trimmed
   and finely chopped

Heat the oil in a frying pan, add the garlic and shallots and cook until golden brown and starting to crisp. Remove from the pan and reserve. Add the chillies to the pan and cook until they start to change colour.

Place the garlic, shallots and chillies in a food processor or blender and blend to a smooth purée with 150 ml/¼ pint water. Pour the purée back into the pan, add the sugar with a large pinch of salt, then cook gently, stirring, until dark in colour. Take care not to burn the mixture.

Pour the stock into a large saucepan, add the garlic purée, rice, lime leaves, soy sauce and the lemon rind and juice. Bring to the boil, then reduce the heat, cover and simmer gently for about 10 minutes.

Add the mushrooms and simmer for a further 10 minutes, or until the mushrooms and rice are tender. Remove the lime leaves, stir in the chopped coriander and ladle into bowls. Place the chopped green chillies and spring onions in small bowls and serve separately to sprinkle on top of the soup.

Try This: FOR AN ALTERNATIVE: 178   FOR A MORE SUBSTANTIAL OPTION: 146

Potato & Fennel Soup

SERVES 4

25 g/1 oz butter
2 large onions, peeled
and thinly sliced
2–3 garlic cloves, peeled
and crushed
1 tsp salt
2 medium potatoes

(about 450 g/1 lb in
weight), peeled and diced
1 fennel bulb, trimmed and
finely chopped
½ tsp caraway seeds
1 litre/1¾ pints
vegetable stock

freshly ground black pepper
2 tbsp freshly chopped
parsley
4 tbsp crème fraîche
roughly torn pieces of
French stick,
to serve

Melt the butter in a large heavy-based saucepan. Add the onions, with the garlic and half the salt, and cook over a medium heat, stirring occasionally, for 7–10 minutes, or until the onions are very soft and beginning to turn brown.

Add the potatoes, fennel bulb, caraway seeds and the remaining salt. Cook for about 5 minutes, then pour in the vegetable stock. Bring to the boil, partially cover and simmer for 15–20 minutes, or until the potatoes are tender. Stir in the chopped parsley and adjust the seasoning to taste.

For a smooth-textured soup, allow to cool slightly then pour into a food processor or blender and blend until smooth. Reheat the soup gently, then ladle into individual soup bowls. For a chunky soup, omit this blending stage and ladle straight from the saucepan into soup bowls.

Swirl a spoonful of crème fraîche into each bowl and serve immediately with roughly-torn pieces of French stick.

Try This: FOR AN ALTERNATIVE: 196   FOR A MORE SUBSTANTIAL OPTION: 152

Potatoes, Leek & Rosemary Soup

SERVES 4

50 g/2 oz butter
450 g/1 lb leeks, trimmed and finely sliced
700 g/1½ lb potatoes, peeled and roughly chopped
900 ml/1½ pints

vegetable stock
4 sprigs of fresh rosemary
450 ml/¾ pint full-cream milk
2 tbsp freshly chopped parsley
2 tbsp crème fraîche

salt and freshly ground black pepper
wholemeal rolls, to serve

Melt the butter in a large saucepan, add the leeks and cook gently for 5 minutes, stirring frequently. Remove 1 tablespoon of the cooked leeks and reserve for garnishing.

Add the potatoes, vegetable stock, rosemary sprigs and milk. Bring to the boil, then reduce the heat, cover and simmer gently for 20–25 minutes, or until the vegetables are tender.

Cool for 10 minutes. Discard the rosemary, then pour into a food processor or blender and blend well to form a smooth-textured soup.

Return the soup to the cleaned saucepan and stir in the chopped parsley and crème fraîche. Season to taste with salt and pepper. If the soup is too thick, stir in a little more milk or water. Reheat gently without boiling, then ladle into warm soup bowls. Garnish the soup with the reserved leeks and serve immediately with wholemeal rolls.

Try This: FOR AN ALTERNATIVE: 194 FOR A MORE SUBSTANTIAL OPTION: 244

Main Meals

Beef Fajitas with Avocado Sauce

SERVES 3-6

2 tbsp sunflower oil
450 g/1 lb beef fillet or rump
  steak, trimmed and cut
  into thin strips
2 garlic cloves, peeled
  and crushed
1 tsp ground cumin
¼ tsp cayenne pepper
1 tbsp paprika

230 g can chopped tomatoes
215 g can red kidney beans,
  drained
1 tbsp freshly
  chopped coriander
1 avocado, peeled, pitted
  and chopped
1 shallot, peeled and
  chopped

1 large tomato, skinned,
  deseeded and chopped
1 red chilli, diced
1 tbsp lemon juice
6 large flour tortilla
  pancakes
3–4 tbsp soured cream
green salad, to serve

Heat the wok, add the oil, then stir-fry the beef for 3–4 minutes. Add the garlic and spices and continue to cook for a further 2 minutes. Stir the tomatoes into the wok, bring to the boil, cover and simmer gently for 5 minutes.

Meanwhile, blend the kidney beans in a food processor until slightly broken up, then add to the wok. Continue to cook for a further 5 minutes, adding 2–3 tablespoons of water. The mixture should be thick and fairly dry. Stir in the chopped coriander.

Mix the chopped avocado, shallot, tomato, chilli and lemon juice together. Spoon into a serving dish and reserve.

When ready to serve, warm the tortillas and spread with a little soured cream. Place a spoonful of the beef mixture on top, followed by a spoonful of the avocado sauce, then roll up. Repeat until all the mixture is used up. Serve immediately with a green salad.

Try This: FOR AN ALTERNATIVE: 88   FOR FINGER FOOD: 34

Honey Pork with
Rice Noodles & Cashews

SERVES 4

125 g/4 oz rice noodles
450 g/1 lb pork fillet
2 tbsp groundnut oil
1 tbsp softened butter
1 onion, peeled and finely
   sliced into rings
2 garlic cloves, peeled

and crushed
125 g/4 oz baby button
   mushrooms, halved
3 tbsp light soy sauce
3 tbsp clear honey
50 g/2 oz unsalted
   cashew nuts

1 red chilli, deseeded
   and finely chopped
4 spring onions, trimmed
   and finely chopped
freshly stir-fried vegetables,
   to serve

Soak the rice noodles in boiling water for 4 minutes or according to packet instructions, then drain and reserve.

Trim and slice the pork fillet into thin strips. Heat the wok, pour in the oil and butter, and stir-fry the pork for 4–5 minutes, until cooked. Remove with a slotted spoon and keep warm.

Add the onion to the wok and stir-fry gently for 2 minutes. Stir in the garlic and mushrooms and cook for a further 2 minutes, or until juices start to run from the mushrooms.

Blend the soy sauce with the honey then return the pork to the wok with this mixture. Add the cashew nuts and cook for 1–2 minutes, then add the rice noodles a little at a time. Stir-fry until everything is piping hot. Sprinkle with chopped chilli and spring onions. Serve immediately with freshly stir-fried vegetables.

Try This: FOR AN ALTERNATIVE: 204   FOR FINGER FOOD: 22

Char Sui Pork & Noodle Salad

SERVES 4

200 g/7 oz flat rice noodles
4 tbsp black treacle
2 tbsp dark soy sauce
3 tbsp Chinese rice wine
　or dry sherry
3 star anise, roughly crushed
1 cinnamon stick
350 g/12 oz pork tenderloin,

in 1 piece
1 tbsp groundnut oil
2 garlic cloves, peeled and
　finely chopped
1 tsp freshly grated
　root ginger
3 spring onions, trimmed
　and sliced

125 g/4 oz pak choi,
　roughly chopped
2 tbsp light soy sauce
fresh coriander leaves,
　to garnish
prepared or bought plum
　sauce, to serve

Preheat the oven to 220°C/425°F/Gas Mark 7, 15 minutes before cooking. Soak the noodles in boiling water according to the packet directions. Drain and reserve. Place the treacle, soy sauce, Chinese rice wine or sherry, star anise and cinnamon into a small saucepan and stir over a gentle heat until mixed thoroughly, then reserve.

Trim the pork tenderloin of any excess fat and put into a shallow dish. Pour the cooled sauce over the tenderloin. Turn the pork, making sure it is completely coated in the sauce. Place in the refrigerator and leave to marinate for 4 hours, turning occasionally.

Remove the pork from its marinade and transfer to a roasting tin. Roast in the preheated oven for 12–14 minutes, basting once, until the pork is cooked through. Remove from the oven and leave until just warm.

Heat the wok, add the oil and when hot, add the garlic, ginger and spring onions. Stir-fry for 30 seconds before adding the pak choi. Stir-fry for a further 1 minute until the pak choi has wilted, then add the noodles and soy sauce. Toss for a few seconds until well mixed, then transfer to a large serving dish. Leave to cool. Thickly slice the pork fillet and add to the cooled noodles. Garnish with coriander leaves and serve with plum sauce.

Try This: FOR AN ALTERNATIVE: 202 FOR FINGER FOOD: 18

Crispy Baked Potatoes
with Serrano Ham

SERVES 4

4 large baking potatoes
4 tsp half-fat crème fraîche
salt and freshly ground
   black pepper
50 g/2 oz lean serrano ham

or prosciutto, with fat
   removed
50 g/2 oz cooked baby
   broad beans
50 g/2 oz cooked carrots, diced

50 g/2 oz cooked peas
50 g/2 oz low-fat hard
   cheese such as Edam
   or Cheddar, grated
fresh green salad, to serve

Preheat the oven to 200°C/400°F/Gas Mark 6. Scrub the potatoes dry. Prick with a fork and place on a baking sheet. Cook for 1–1½ hours or until tender when squeezed. (Use oven gloves or a kitchen towel to pick up the potatoes as they will be very hot.)

Cut the potatoes in half horizontally and scoop out all the flesh into a bowl. Spoon the crème fraîche into the bowl and mix thoroughly with the potatoes. Season to taste with a little salt and pepper.

Cut the ham into strips and carefully stir into the potato mixture with the broad beans, carrots and peas. Pile the mixture back into the 8 potato shells and sprinkle a little grated cheese on the top.

Place under a hot grill and cook until golden and heated through. Serve immediately with a fresh green salad.

Try This: FOR AN ALTERNATIVE: 282   FOR FINGER FOOD: 82

Stuffed Tomatoes
with Grilled Polenta

SERVES 4

For the polenta:
300 ml/½ pint
vegetable stock
salt and freshly ground
black pepper
50 g/2 oz quick-cook polenta
15 g/½ oz butter

For the stuffed tomatoes:
4 large tomatoes
1 tbsp olive oil
1 garlic clove, peeled and
crushed
1 bunch spring onions,
trimmed and finely
chopped

2 tbsp freshly
chopped parsley
2 tbsp freshly chopped basil
2 slices Parma ham, cut into
thin slivers
50 g/2 oz fresh white
breadcrumbs
snipped chives, to garnish

Preheat grill just before cooking. To make the polenta, pour the stock into a saucepan. Add a pinch of salt and bring to the boil. Pour in the polenta in a fine stream, stirring all the time. Simmer for about 15 minutes, or until very thick. Stir in the butter and add a little pepper. Turn the polenta out on to a chopping board and spread to a thickness of just over 1 cm/½ inch. Cool, cover with clingfilm and chill in the refrigerator for 30 minutes.

To make the stuffed tomatoes, cut the tomatoes in half then scoop out the seeds and press through a fine sieve to extract the juices. Season the insides of the tomatoes with salt and pepper and reserve. Heat the olive oil in a saucepan and gently fry the garlic and spring onions for 3 minutes. Add the tomatoes' juices, and bubble for 3–4 minutes, or until most of the liquid has evaporated. Stir in the herbs, Parma ham and a little black pepper with half the breadcrumbs. Spoon into the hollowed-out tomatoes and reserve.

Cut the polenta into 5 cm/2 inch squares, then cut each in half diagonally to make triangles. Put the triangles on a piece of tinfoil on the grill rack and grill for 4–5 minutes on each side, until golden. Cover and keep warm. Grill the tomatoes under a medium-hot grill for about 4 minutes – any exposed Parma ham will become crisp. Sprinkle with the remaining breadcrumbs and grill for 1–2 minutes, or until the breadcrumbs are golden brown. Garnish with snipped chives and serve immediately with the grilled polenta.

Try This: FOR AN ALTERNATIVE: 260   FOR FINGER FOOD: 78

Penne with Mixed Peppers & Garlic

SERVES 4

450 g/1 lb green, red and
  yellow peppers
2 tbsp olive oil
1 large onion,
  peeled and sliced
1 celery stick, trimmed
  and finely chopped
2 garlic cloves, peeled

and crushed
4 rashers smoked streaky
  bacon, finely chopped
300 ml/½ pint chicken stock
salt and freshly ground
  black pepper
350 g/12 oz fresh penne
2 tbsp freshly

chopped parsley
2 tbsp pecorino cheese,
  finely grated

To serve:
green salad
warm granary bread

Preheat the grill and line the grill rack with tinfoil. Cut the peppers in half, deseed and place cut side down on the grill rack. Cook under the grill until the skins become blistered and black all over. Place the peppers in a polythene bag and allow to cool, then discard the skin and slice thinly.

Heat the oil in a heavy-based pan. Add the onion, celery, garlic and bacon and cook for 4–5 minutes, or until the onion has softened. Add the peppers and cook for 1 minute. Pour in the stock and season to taste with salt and pepper. Cover and simmer for 20 minutes.

Meanwhile, bring a large pan of lightly salted water to a rolling boil. Add the penne and cook according to the packet instructions, about 3–4 minutes, or until 'al dente'. Drain thoroughly and return to the pan.

Pour the pepper sauce over the pasta and toss lightly. Tip into a warmed serving dish and sprinkle with the chopped parsley and grated pecorino cheese. Serve immediately with a green salad and warm granary bread.

Try This: FOR AN ALTERNATIVE: 122   FOR FINGER FOOD: 78

Stir–fried Lemon Chicken

SERVES 4

350 g/12 oz boneless,
   skinless chicken breast
1 large egg white
5 tsp cornflour
3 tbsp vegetable or
   groundnut oil
150 ml/1⁄4 pint chicken stock

2 tbsp fresh lemon juice
2 tbsp light soy sauce
1 tbsp Chinese rice wine or
   dry sherry
1 tbsp sugar
2 garlic cloves, peeled and
   finely chopped

1⁄4 tsp dried chilli flakes,
   or to taste

To garnish:
lemon rind strips
red chilli slices

Using a sharp knife, trim the chicken, discarding any fat and cut into thin strips, about 5 cm/2 inch long and 1 cm/½ inch wide. Place in a shallow dish. Lightly whisk the egg white and 1 tablespoon of the cornflour together until smooth. Pour over the chicken strips and mix well until coated evenly. Leave to marinate in the refrigerator for at least 20 minutes.

When ready to cook, drain the chicken and reserve. Heat a wok or large frying pan, add the oil and when hot, add the chicken and stir-fry for 1–2 minutes, or until the chicken has turned white. Using a slotted spoon, remove from the wok and reserve.

Wipe the wok clean and return to the heat. Add the chicken stock, lemon juice, soy sauce, Chinese rice wine or sherry, sugar, garlic and chilli flakes and bring to the boil. Blend the remaining cornflour with 1 tablespoon of water and stir into the stock. Simmer for 1 minute.

Return the chicken to the wok and continue simmering for a further 2–3 minutes, or until the chicken is tender and the sauce has thickened. Garnish with lemon strips and red chilli slices. Serve immediately.

Try This: FOR AN ALTERNATIVE: 214   FOR FINGER FOOD: 30

Pan-cooked Chicken with Thai Spices

SERVES 4

4 kaffir lime leaves
5 cm/2 inch piece of root
    ginger, peeled and
    chopped
300 ml/½ pint chicken
    stock, boiling
4 x 175 g/6 oz
    chicken breasts

2 tsp groundnut oil
5 tbsp coconut milk
1 tbsp fish sauce
2 red chillies, deseeded and
    finely chopped
225 g/8 oz Thai jasmine rice
1 tbsp lime juice
3 tbsp freshly

    chopped coriander
salt and freshly ground
    black pepper

To garnish:
wedges of lime
freshly chopped coriander

Lightly bruise the kaffir lime leaves and put in a bowl with the chopped ginger. Pour over the chicken stock, cover and leave to infuse for 30 minutes.

Meanwhile, cut each chicken breast into two pieces. Heat the oil in a large, non-stick frying pan or flameproof casserole and brown the chicken pieces for 2–3 minutes on each side.

Strain the infused chicken stock into the pan. Half cover the pan with a lid and gently simmer for 10 minutes.

Stir in the coconut milk, fish sauce and chopped chillies. Simmer, uncovered for 5–6 minutes, or until the chicken is tender and cooked through and the sauce has reduced slightly.

Meanwhile, cook the rice in boiling salted water according to the packet instructions. Drain the rice thoroughly.

Stir the lime juice and chopped coriander into the sauce. Season to taste with salt and pepper. Serve the chicken and sauce on a bed of rice. Garnish with wedges of lime and freshly chopped coriander and serve immediately.

Try This: FOR AN ALTERNATIVE: 212   FOR FINGER FOOD: 30

Thai Stir-fried Spicy Turkey

SERVES 4

2 tbsp Thai fragrant rice
2 tbsp lemon juice
3–5 tbsp chicken stock
2 tbsp Thai fish sauce
½–1 tsp cayenne pepper, or
   to taste

125 g/4 oz fresh turkey mince
2 shallots, peeled
   and chopped
½ lemon grass stalk, outer
   leaves discarded and
   finely sliced

1 lime leaf, finely sliced
1 spring onion, trimmed
   and finely chopped
freshly chopped coriander,
   to garnish
Chinese leaves, to serve

Place the rice in a small frying pan and cook, stirring constantly, over a medium high heat for 4–5 minutes, or until the rice is browned. Transfer to a spice grinder or blender and pulse briefly until roughly ground. Reserve.

Place the lemon juice, 3 tablespoons of the stock, the fish sauce and cayenne pepper into a small saucepan and bring to the boil. Add the turkey mince and return to the boil. Continue cooking over a high heat until the turkey is sealed all over.

Add the shallots to the saucepan with the lemon grass, lime leaf, spring onion and reserved rice. Continue cooking for another 1–2 minutes, or until the turkey is cooked through, adding a little more stock, if necessary, to keep the mixture moist.

Spoon a little of the mixture into each Chinese leaf and arrange on a serving dish or individual plates. Garnish with a little chopped coriander and serve immediately.

Try This: FOR AN ALTERNATIVE: 218　FOR FINGER FOOD: 38

Turkey Escalopes with Apricot Chutney

SERVES 4

4 x 175–225 g/6–8 oz
   turkey steaks
1 tbsp plain flour
salt and freshly ground
   black pepper
1 tbsp olive oil
flat-leaf parsley sprigs,
   to garnish

orange wedges,
   to serve

For the apricot chutney:
125 g/4 oz no-need-to-soak
   dried apricots, chopped
1 red onion, peeled and
   finely chopped

1 tsp grated fresh root ginger
2 tbsp caster sugar
finely grated rind of
   ½ orange
125 ml/4 fl oz fresh
   orange juice
125 ml/4 fl oz ruby port
1 whole clove

Put a turkey steak on to a sheet of non-pvc clingfilm or non-stick baking parchment. Cover with a second sheet. Using a rolling pin, gently pound the turkey until the meat is flattened to about 5 mm/¼ inch thick. Repeat to make 4 escalopes.

Mix the flour with the salt and pepper and use to lightly dust the turkey escalopes.

Put the turkey escalopes on a board or baking tray and cover with a piece of non-pvc clingfilm or non-stick baking parchment. Chill in the refrigerator until ready to cook.

For the apricot chutney, put the apricots, onion, ginger, sugar, orange rind, orange juice, port and clove into a saucepan. Slowly bring to the boil and simmer, uncovered for 10 minutes, stirring occasionally, until thick and syrupy. Remove the clove and stir in the chopped coriander.

Heat the oil in a pan and chargriddle the turkey escalopes, in two batches if necessary, for 3–4 minutes on each side until golden brown and tender.

Spoon the chutney on to four individual serving plates. Place a turkey escalope on top of each spoonful of chutney. Garnish with sprigs of parsley and serve immediately with orange wedges.

Try This: FOR AN ALTERNATIVE: 216 FOR FINGER FOOD: 30

Duck in Crispy Wonton Shells

SERVES 4

2 x 175 g/6 oz duck breasts
2 tbsp Chinese five
  spice powder
2 tbsp Sichuan peppercorns
1 tsp whole black
  peppercorns

3 tbsp cumin seeds
5 tbsp sea salt
6 slices fresh root ginger
6 spring onions, roughly
  chopped
1 tbsp cornflour

1 litre/1¾ pints vegetable oil
  for frying
16 wonton wrappers
5 cm/2 inch piece cucumber,
  cut into fine strips
125 ml/4 fl oz hoisin sauce

Rinse the duck and dry thoroughly with absorbent kitchen paper. Place the Chinese five spice powder, peppercorns, cumin seeds and salt in a pestle and mortar and crush. Rub the spice mix all over the duck. Wrap in clingfilm and refrigerate for 24 hours.

Place a rack in the wok and pour in boiling water to a depth of 5 cm/2 inches. Place the duck breasts with the ginger slices and 3 chopped spring onions in a heatproof dish on top of the rack. Cover and steam for 40–50 minutes, or until the duck is cooked. Pour off any excess fat from time to time and add more water if necessary. Remove the duck and leave until cooled.

Dust the duck breasts with cornflour, shaking off the excess. Heat the wok, add the oil and, when almost smoking, deep-fry the duck for 8 minutes. Drain, then shred the meat into bite-sized pieces. Shred the remaining spring onions.

Reheat the oil until smoking. Working with 1 wonton at a time, insert 2 wooden skewers into each one, hold in a taco shape and lower into the oil. Hold in the oil until crisp and golden brown. Drain on absorbent kitchen paper. Repeat with the remaining wontons. Fill the wontons with the duck, topped with the spring onions, cucumber and hoisin sauce and serve immediately.

Try This: FOR AN ALTERNATIVE: 222   FOR FINGER FOOD: 38

Brown Rice & Lentil Salad with Duck

SERVES 6

225 g/8 oz Puy lentils, rinsed
4 tbsp olive oil
1 medium onion, peeled and
  finely chopped
200 g/7 oz long-grain
  brown rice
½ tsp dried thyme
450 ml/¾ pint chicken stock
salt and freshly ground
  black pepper
350 g/12 oz shiitake or
  portabella mushrooms,
  trimmed and sliced

375 g/13 oz cooked Chinese-
  style spicy duck or
  roasted duck, sliced
  into chunks
2 garlic cloves, peeled and
  finely chopped
125 g/4 oz cooked smoked
  ham, diced
2 small courgettes, trimmed,
  diced and blanched
6 spring onions, trimmed
  and thinly sliced
2 tbsp freshly chopped

parsley
2 tbsp walnut halves,
  toasted and chopped

For the dressing:
2 tbsp red or white
  wine vinegar
1 tbsp balsamic vinegar
1 tsp Dijon mustard
1 tsp clear honey
75 ml/3 fl oz extra-virgin
  olive oil
2–3 tbsp walnut oil

Bring a large saucepan of water to the boil, sprinkle in the lentils, return to the boil, then simmer over a low heat for 30 minutes, or until tender; do not overcook. Drain and rinse under cold running water, then drain again and reserve.

Heat 2 tablespoons of the oil in a saucepan. Add the onion and cook for 2 minutes until it begins to soften. Stir in the rice with the thyme and stock. Season to taste with salt and pepper and bring to the boil. Cover and simmer for 40 minutes, or until tender and the liquid is absorbed.

Heat the remaining oil in a large frying pan and add the mushrooms. Cook for 5 minutes until golden. Stir in the duck and garlic and cook for 2–3 minutes to heat through. Season well.

To make the dressing, whisk the vinegars, mustard and honey in a large serving bowl, then gradually whisk in the oils. Add the lentils and the rice, then stir lightly together. Gently stir in the ham, blanched courgettes, spring onions and parsley. Season to taste and sprinkle with the walnuts. Serve topped with the duck and mushrooms.

Try This: FOR AN ALTERNATIVE: 220   FOR FINGER FOOD: 36

Thai Prawn & Rice Noodle Salad

SERVES 4

75 g/3 oz rice vermicelli
175 g/6 oz mangetout, cut in
   half crossways
½ cucumber, peeled,
   deseeded and diced
2–3 spring onions, trimmed
   and thinly sliced
   diagonally
16–20 large cooked tiger
   prawns, peeled with tails

left on
2 tbsp chopped unsalted
   peanuts or cashews

For the dressing:
4 tbsp freshly squeezed
   lime juice
3 tbsp Thai fish sauce
1 tbsp sugar
2.5 cm/1 inch piece fresh

root ginger, peeled and
   finely chopped
1 red chilli, deseeded and
   thinly sliced
3–4 tbsp freshly chopped
   coriander or mint

To garnish:
lime wedges
sprigs of fresh mint

Place the vermicelli in a bowl and pour over hot water to cover. Leave to stand for 5 minutes or until softened. Drain, rinse, then drain again and reserve.

Meanwhile, mix all the dressing ingredients in a large bowl until well blended and the sugar has dissolved. Reserve.

Bring a medium saucepan of water to the boil. Add the mangetout, return to the boil and cook for 30–50 seconds. Drain, refresh under cold running water, drain again and reserve.

Stir the cucumber, spring onions and all but 4 of the prawns into the dressing until coated lightly. Add the mangetout and noodles and toss until all the ingredients are mixed evenly.

Spoon the noodle salad on to warmed individual plates. Sprinkle with peanuts or cashews and garnish each dish with a reserved prawn, a lime wedge and a sprig of mint.

Try This: FOR AN ALTERNATIVE: 226   FOR FINGER FOOD: 44

Szechuan Chilli Prawns

SERVES 4

450 g/1 lb raw tiger prawns
2 tbsp groundnut oil
1 onion, peeled and sliced
1 red pepper, deseeded and
   cut into strips
1 small red chilli, deseeded
   and thinly sliced
2 garlic cloves, peeled and

finely chopped
2–3 spring onions, trimmed
   and diagonally sliced
freshly cooked rice or
   noodles, to serve
sprigs of fresh coriander
   or chilli flowers,
   to garnish

For the chilli sauce:
1 tbsp cornflour
4 tbsp cold fish stock
   or water
2 tbsp soy sauce
2 tbsp sweet or hot chilli
   sauce, or to taste
2 tsp soft light brown sugar

Peel the prawns, leaving the tails attached if you like. Using a sharp knife, remove the black vein along the back of the prawns. Rinse and pat dry with absorbent kitchen paper.

Heat a wok or large frying pan, add the oil and, when hot, add the onion, pepper and chilli and stir-fry for 4–5 minutes, or until the vegetables are tender but retain a bite. Stir in the garlic and cook for 30 seconds. Using a slotted spoon, transfer to a plate and reserve.

Add the prawns to the wok and stir-fry for 1–2 minutes, or until they turn pink and opaque.

Blend all the chilli sauce ingredients together in a bowl or jug, then stir into the prawns. Add the reserved vegetables and bring to the boil, stirring constantly. Cook for 1–2 minutes, or until the sauce is thickened and the prawns and vegetables are well coated.

Stir in the spring onions, tip on to a warmed platter and garnish with chilli flowers or coriander sprigs. Serve immediately with freshly cooked rice or noodles.

Try This: FOR AN ALTERNATIVE: 224   FOR FINGER FOOD: 48

Salmon Noisettes with Fruity Sauce

SERVES 4

4 x 125 g/4 oz salmon steaks
grated rind and juice of
  2 lemons
grated rind and juice
  of 1 lime
3 tbsp olive oil

1 tbsp clear honey
1 tbsp wholegrain mustard
coarse sea salt and freshly
  ground black pepper
1 tbsp groundnut oil
125 g/4 oz mixed salad

leaves, washed
1 bunch watercress, washed
  and thick stalks removed
250 g/9 oz baby plum
  tomatoes, halved

Using a sharp knife, cut the bone away from each salmon steak to create 2 salmon fillets. Repeat with the remaining salmon steaks. Shape the salmon fillets into noisettes and secure with fine string.

Mix together the citrus rinds and juices, olive oil, honey, wholegrain mustard, salt and pepper in a shallow dish. Add the salmon fillets and turn to coat. Cover and leave to marinate in the refrigerator for 4 hours, turning them occasionally in the marinade.

Heat the wok then add the groundnut oil and heat until hot. Lift out the salmon noisettes, reserving the marinade. Add the salmon to the wok and cook for 6–10 minutes, turning once during cooking, until cooked and the fish is just flaking. Pour the marinade into the wok and heat through gently.

Mix together the salad leaves, watercress and tomatoes and arrange on serving plates. Top with the salmon noisettes and drizzle over any remaining warm marinade. Serve immediately.

Try This: FOR AN ALTERNATIVE: 236   FOR FINGER FOOD: 58

Potato Pancakes with Smoked Salmon

SERVES 4

450 g/1 lb floury potatoes,
  peeled and quartered
salt and freshly ground
  black pepper
1 large egg
1 large egg yolk
25 g/1 oz butter

25 g/1 oz plain flour
150 ml/¼ pint double cream
2 tbsp freshly chopped
  parsley
5 tbsp crème fraîche
1 tbsp horseradish sauce
225 g/8 oz smoked

salmon, sliced
salad leaves,
  to serve

To garnish:
lemon slices
snipped chives

Cook the potatoes in a saucepan of lightly salted boiling water for 15–20 minutes, or until tender. Drain thoroughly, then mash until free of lumps. Beat in the whole egg and egg yolk, together with the butter. Beat until smooth and creamy. Slowly beat in the flour and cream, then season to taste with salt and pepper. Stir in the chopped parsley.

Beat the crème fraîche and horseradish sauce together in a small bowl, cover with cling-film and reserve.

Heat a lightly oiled, heavy-based frying pan over a medium-high heat. Place a few spoonfuls of the potato mixture in the hot pan and cook for 4–5 minutes, or until cooked and golden, turning halfway through cooking time. Remove from the pan, drain on absorbent kitchen paper and keep warm. Repeat with the remaining mixture.

Arrange the pancakes on individual serving plates. Place the smoked salmon on the pancakes and spoon over a little of the horseradish sauce. Serve with salad and the remaining horseradish sauce and garnish with lemon slices and chives.

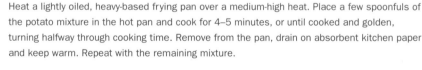

Try This: FOR AN ALTERNATIVE: 232   FOR FINGER FOOD: 56

Stir–fried Salmon with Peas

SERVES 4

450 g/1 lb salmon fillet
salt
6 slices streaky bacon
1 tbsp vegetable oil
50 ml/2 fl oz chicken
   or fish stock

2 tbsp dark soy sauce
2 tbsp Chinese rice wine or
   dry sherry
1 tsp sugar
75 g/3 oz frozen peas, thawed
1–2 tbsp freshly

   shredded mint
1 tsp cornflour
sprigs of fresh mint,
   to garnish
freshly cooked noodles,
   to serve

Wipe and skin the salmon fillet and remove any pin bones. Slice into 2.5 cm/1 inch strips, place on a plate and sprinkle with salt. Leave for 20 minutes, then pat dry with absorbent kitchen paper and reserve. Remove any cartilage from the bacon, cut into small dice and reserve.

Heat a wok or large frying pan over a high heat, then add the oil and when hot, add the bacon and stir-fry for 3 minutes or until crisp and golden. Push to one side and add the strips of salmon. Stir fry gently for 2 minutes or until the flesh is opaque.

Pour the chicken or fish stock, soy sauce and Chinese rice wine or sherry into the wok, then stir in the sugar, peas and freshly shredded mint.

Blend the cornflour with 1 tablespoon of water to form a smooth paste and stir into the sauce. Bring to the boil, reduce the heat and simmer for 1 minute, or until slightly thickened and smooth. Garnish and serve immediately with noodles.

Try This: FOR AN ALTERNATIVE: 234   FOR FINGER FOOD: 54

Teriyaki Salmon

SERVES 4

450 g/1 lb salmon fillet, skinned
6 tbsp Japanese teriyaki sauce
1 tbsp rice wine vinegar
1 tbsp tomato paste

dash of Tabasco sauce
grated zest of ½ lemon
salt and freshly ground black pepper
4 tbsp groundnut oil
1 carrot, peeled and cut into

matchsticks
125 g/4 oz mangetout peas
125 g/4 oz oyster mushrooms, wiped

Using a sharp knife, cut the salmon into thick slices and place in a shallow dish. Mix together the teriyaki sauce, rice wine vinegar, tomato paste, Tabasco sauce, lemon zest and seasoning. Spoon the marinade over the salmon, then cover loosely and leave to marinate in the refrigerator for 30 minutes, turning the salmon or spooning the marinade occasionally over the salmon.

Heat a large wok, then add 2 tablespoons of the oil until almost smoking. Stir fry the carrot for 2 minutes, then add the mangetout peas and stir-fry for a further 2 minutes. Add the oyster mushrooms and stir-fry for 4 minutes, until softened. Using a slotted spoon, transfer the vegetables to 4 warmed serving plates and keep warm.

Remove the salmon from the marinade, reserving both the salmon and marinade. Add the remaining oil to the wok, heat until almost smoking, then cook the salmon for 4–5 minutes, turning once during cooking, or until the fish is just flaking. Add the marinade and heat through for 1 minute. Serve immediately, with the salmon arranged on top of the vegetables and the marinade drizzled over.

Try This: FOR AN ALTERNATIVE: 242   FOR FINGER FOOD: 42

Salmon with Strawberry Sauce

SERVES 4

4 x 150 g/5 oz salmon fillets
25 g/1 oz butter
2 tbsp groundnut oil
1 dessert apple, cored and
   cut into chunks
1 bunch spring onions,
   trimmed and diagonally
   sliced

1 garlic clove,
   peeled and sliced
50 g/2 oz pine nuts
juice of 1 lemon
125 g/4 oz strawberries,
   hulled and halved
1 bunch basil, freshly
   chopped

salt and freshly ground
   black pepper

To serve:
freshly cooked creamy
   mashed potatoes
freshly cooked broad beans

Wash the salmon fillets and pat dry on absorbent kitchen paper. Heat the wok, then add the butter and half the oil and heat until bubbling. Cook the salmon fillets flesh side down for 5 minutes, until they are sealed. Then, using a fish slice, carefully turn the salmon fillets over and cook for a further 3–5 minutes, until the salmon flesh is just flaking.

Transfer the salmon fillets to warmed serving plates and keep warm in a low oven. Wipe the wok clean, then add the remaining oil to the wok and heat until almost smoking.

Add the apple chunks, spring onions, garlic slices and pine nuts and cook for 5 minutes, stirring occasionally, until they are golden brown.

Stir in the lemon juice, strawberries, chopped basil and season to taste with salt and pepper. Heat through thoroughly.

Spoon the sauce over the salmon fillets and serve immediately with creamy mashed potatoes and freshly cooked broad beans.

Try This: FOR AN ALTERNATIVE: 228   FOR FINGER FOOD: 56

Barbecued Fish Kebabs

SERVES 4

450 g/1 lb herring
  or mackerel fillets,
  cut into chunks
2 small red onions,
  peeled and quartered
16 cherry tomatoes

salt and freshly ground
  black pepper

For the sauce:
150 ml /¼ pint fish stock
5 tbsp tomato ketchup

2 tbsp Worcestershire sauce
2 tbsp wine vinegar
2 tbsp brown sugar
2 drops Tabasco
2 tbsp tomato purée

Line a grill rack with a single layer of tinfoil and preheat the grill at a high temperature, 2 minutes before use. If using wooden skewers, soak in cold water for 30 minutes to prevent them from catching alight during cooking.

Meanwhile, prepare the sauce. Add the fish stock, tomato ketchup, Worcestershire sauce, vinegar, sugar, Tabasco and tomato purée to a small saucepan. Stir well and leave to simmer for 5 minutes.

When ready to cook, drain the skewers, if necessary, then thread the fish chunks, the quartered red onions and the cherry tomatoes alternately on to the skewers.

Season the kebabs to taste with salt and pepper and brush with the sauce. Grill under the preheated grill for 8–10 minutes, basting with the sauce occasionally during cooking. Turn the kebabs often to ensure that they are cooked thoroughly and evenly on all sides. Serve immediately with couscous.

Try This: FOR AN ALTERNATIVE: 240   FOR FINGER FOOD: 58

Sardines with Redcurrants

SERVES 4

2 tbsp redcurrant jelly
finely grated rind of 1 lime
2 tbsp medium dry sherry
450 g /1 lb fresh
   sardines, cleaned

and heads removed
sea salt and freshly ground
   black pepper
fresh redcurrants, to garnish

To serve:
lime wedges
fresh green salad

Preheat the grill and line the grill rack with tinfoil 2–3 minutes before cooking.

Warm the redcurrant jelly in a bowl standing over a pan of gently simmering water and stir until smooth. Add the lime rind and sherry to the bowl and stir well until blended.

Lightly rinse the sardines and pat dry with absorbent kitchen paper. Place on a chopping board and with a sharp knife make several diagonal cuts across the flesh of each fish. Season the sardines inside the cavities with salt and pepper.

Gently brush the warm marinade over the skin and inside the cavities of the sardines.

Place on the grill rack and cook under the preheated grill for 8–10 minutes, or until the fish are cooked. Carefully turn the sardines over at least once during grilling. Baste occasionally with the remaining redcurrant and lime marinade. Garnish with the redcurrants. Serve immediately with the salad and lime wedges.

Try This: FOR AN ALTERNATIVE: 236   FOR FINGER FOOD: 58

Hot Salsa–filled Sole

SERVES 4

8 x 175 g/6 oz lemon
   sole fillets, skinned
150 ml/¼ pint orange juice
2 tbsp lemon juice

For the salsa:
1 small mango

8 cherry tomatoes,
   quartered
1 small red onion, peeled
   and finely chopped
pinch of sugar
1 red chilli
2 tbsp rice vinegar

zest and juice of 1 lime
1 tbsp olive oil
sea salt and freshly ground
   black pepper
2 tbsp freshly chopped mint
lime wedges, to garnish
salad leaves, to serve

First make the salsa. Peel the mango and cut the flesh away from the stone. Chop finely and place in a small bowl. Add the cherry tomatoes to the mango together with the onion and sugar.

Cut the top off the chilli. Slit down the side and discard the seeds and the membrane (the skin to which the seeds are attached). Finely chop the chilli and add to the mango mixture with the vinegar, lime zest, juice and oil. Season to taste with salt and pepper. Mix thoroughly and leave to stand for 30 minutes to allow the flavours to develop.

Lay the fish fillets on a board skinned-side up and pile the salsa on the tail-end of the fillets. Fold the fillets in half, season and place in a large shallow frying pan. Pour over the orange and lemon juice.

Bring to a gentle boil, then reduce the heat to a simmer. Cover and cook on a low heat for 7–10 minutes, adding a little water if the liquid is evaporating. Remove the cover, add the mint and cook uncovered for a further 3 minutes. Garnish with lime wedges and serve immediately with the salad.

Try This: FOR AN ALTERNATIVE: 246   FOR FINGER FOOD: 56

Smoked Mackerel & Potato Salad

SERVES 4

½ tsp dry mustard powder
1 large egg yolk
salt and freshly ground
    black pepper
150 ml/¼ pint sunflower oil
1–2 tbsp lemon juice

450 g/1 lb baby new
    potatoes
25 g/1 oz butter
350 g/12 oz smoked
    mackerel fillets
4 celery stalks, trimmed and

    finely chopped
3 tbsp creamed horseradish
150 ml/¼ pint crème fraîche
1 Little Gem lettuce, rinsed
    and roughly torn
8 cherry tomatoes, halved

Place the mustard powder and egg yolk in a small bowl with salt and pepper and whisk until blended. Add the oil, drop by drop, into the egg mixture, whisking continuously. When the mayonnaise is thick, add the lemon juice, drop by drop, until a smooth, glossy consistency is formed. Reserve.

Cook the potatoes in boiling salted water until tender, then drain. Cool slightly, then cut into halves or quarters, depending on size. Return to the saucepan and toss in the butter.

Remove the skin from the mackerel fillets and flake into pieces. Add to the potatoes in the saucepan, together with the celery.

Blend 4 tablespoons of the mayonnaise with the horseradish and crème fraîche. Season to taste with salt and pepper, then add to the potato and mackerel mixture and stir lightly.

Arrange the lettuce and tomatoes on 4 serving plates. Pile the smoked mackerel mixture on top of the lettuce, grind over a little pepper and serve with the remaining mayonnaise.

 Try This: FOR AN ALTERNATIVE: 228   FOR FINGER FOOD: 54

Spicy Cod Rice

SERVES 4

1 tbsp plain flour
1 tbsp freshly chopped
 coriander
1 tsp ground cumin
1 tsp ground coriander
550 g/1¼ lb thick-cut cod
 fillet, skinned and cut
 into large chunks

4 tbsp groundnut oil
50 g/2 oz cashew nuts
1 bunch spring onions,
 trimmed and diagonally
 sliced
1 red chilli, deseeded and
 chopped
1 carrot, peeled and cut

into matchsticks
125 g/4 oz frozen peas
450 g/1 lb cooked long-grain
 rice
2 tbsp sweet chilli sauce
2 tbsp soy sauce

Mix together the flour, coriander, cumin and ground coriander on a large plate. Coat the cod in the spice mixture then place on a baking sheet, cover and chill in the refrigerator for 30 minutes.

Heat a large wok, then add 2 tablespoons of the oil and heat until almost smoking. Stir-fry the cashew nuts for 1 minute, until browned, then remove and reserve.

Add a further 1 tablespoon of the oil and heat until almost smoking. Add the cod and stir-fry for 2 minutes. Using a fish slice, turn the cod pieces over and cook for a further 2 minutes, until golden. Remove from the wok, place on a warm plate, cover and keep warm.

Add the remaining oil to the wok, heat until almost smoking then stir-fry the spring onions and chilli for 1 minute before adding the carrots and peas and stir-frying for a further 2 minutes. Stir in the rice, chilli sauce, soy sauce and cashew nuts and stir-fry for 3 more minutes. Add the cod, heat for 1 minute, then serve immediately.

Try This: FOR AN ALTERNATIVE: 250   FOR FINGER FOOD: 64

Spaghetti alla Puttanesca

SERVES 4

4 tbsp olive oil
50 g/2 oz anchovy fillets in
   olive oil, drained and
   coarsely chopped
2 garlic cloves, peeled and
   finely chopped
½ tsp crushed dried chillies

400 g can chopped
   plum tomatoes
125 g/4 oz pitted black
   olives, cut in half
2 tbsp capers,
   rinsed and drained
1 tsp freshly chopped

oregano
1 tbsp tomato paste
salt and freshly ground
   black pepper
400 g/14 oz spaghetti
2 tbsp freshly
   chopped parsley

Heat the olive oil in a large frying pan, add the anchovies and cook, stirring with a wooden spoon and crushing the anchovies, until they disintegrate. Add the garlic and dried chillies and cook for 1 minute, stirring frequently.

Add the tomatoes, olives, capers, oregano and tomato paste and cook, stirring occasionally, for 15 minutes, or until the liquid has evaporated and the sauce is thickened. Season the tomato sauce to taste with salt and pepper.

Meanwhile, bring a large pan of lightly salted water to a rolling boil. Add the spaghetti and cook according to the packet instructions, or until 'al dente'.

Drain the spaghetti thoroughly, reserving 1–2 tablespoons of the the cooking water. Return the spaghetti with the reserved water to the pan. Pour the tomato sauce over the spaghetti, add the chopped parsley and toss to coat. Tip into a warmed serving dish or spoon on to individual plates and serve immediately.

Try This: FOR AN ALTERNATIVE: 268   FOR FINGER FOOD: 76

Spiced Tomato Pilau

SERVES 2-3

225 g/8 oz basmati rice
40 g/1½ oz unsalted butter
4 green cardamom pods
2 star anise
4 whole cloves
10 black peppercorns

5 cm/2 inch piece
  cinnamon stick
1 large red onion, peeled
  and finely sliced
175 g/6 oz canned
  chopped tomatoes

salt and freshly ground
  black pepper
sprigs of fresh coriander,
  to garnish

Wash the rice in several changes of water until the water remains relatively clear. Drain the rice and cover with fresh water. Leave to soak for 30 minutes. Drain well and reserve.

Heat the wok, then melt the butter and add the cardamoms, star anise, cloves, black peppercorns and the cinnamon stick. Cook gently for 30 seconds. Increase the heat and add the onion. Stir-fry for 7–8 minutes until tender and starting to brown. Add the drained rice and cook a further 2–3 minutes.

Sieve the tomatoes and mix with sufficient warm water to make 450 ml/16 fl oz. Pour this into the wok, season to taste with salt and pepper and bring to the boil.

Cover, reduce the heat to very low and cook for 10 minutes. Remove the wok from the heat and leave covered for a further 10 minutes. Do not lift the lid during cooking or resting. Finally, uncover and mix well with a fork, heat for 1 minute, then garnish with the sprigs of fresh coriander and serve immediately.

Try This: FOR AN ALTERNATIVE: 246   FOR FINGER FOOD: 64

Crispy Noodle Salad

SERVES 4

2 tbsp sunflower seeds
2 tbsp pumpkin seeds
50 g/2 oz rice vermicelli
  or stir-fry noodles
175 g/6 oz unsalted butter
2 tbsp sesame seeds,
  lightly toasted

125 g/4 oz red cabbage,
  trimmed and shredded
1 orange pepper, deseeded
  and finely chopped
125 g/4 oz button
  mushrooms, wiped
  and quartered

2 spring onions, trimmed
  and finely chopped
salt and freshly ground
  black pepper
shredded pickled sushi
  ginger, to garnish

Preheat the oven to 200°C/400°F/Gas Mark 6, then sprinkle the sunflower and pumpkin seeds on a baking sheet. Toast in the oven, stirring occasionally, for 10–15 minutes or until lightly toasted. Remove from the oven and leave to cool.

Crush the rice vermicelli into small pieces (this is easiest in a plastic bag or while the noodles are still in the packet), and reserve. Melt the butter in a small saucepan and leave to cool for a few minutes. Pour the clear yellow liquid carefully into a bowl, leaving behind the white milky solids. Discard the milky solids.

Heat the yellow, clarified butter in a wok and fry the crushed noodles in batches until browned, stirring constantly and gently. Remove the fried noodles as they cook, using a slotted spoon, and drain on absorbent kitchen paper. Transfer the noodles to a bowl and add the toasted seeds.

Mix together the red cabbage, orange pepper, button mushrooms and spring onions in a large bowl and season to taste with salt and pepper. Just before serving, add the noodles and seeds to the salad and mix gently. Garnish with a little sushi ginger and serve.

Try This: FOR AN ALTERNATIVE: 286   FOR FINGER FOOD: 70

Spicy Cucumber Stir Fry

SERVES 4

25 g/1 oz black soya beans,
   soaked in cold water,
   overnight
1½ cucumbers
2 tsp salt

1 tbsp groundnut oil
½ tsp mild chilli powder
4 garlic cloves,
   peeled and crushed
5 tbsp chicken stock

1 tsp sesame oil
1 tbsp freshly
   chopped parsley,
   to garnish

Rinse the soaked beans thoroughly, then drain. Place in a saucepan, cover with cold water and bring to the boil, skimming off any scum that rises to the surface. Boil for 10 minutes, then reduce the heat and simmer for 1–1½ hours. Drain and reserve.

Peel the cucumbers, slice lengthways and remove the seeds. Cut into 2.5 cm/1 inch slices and place in a colander over a bowl. Sprinkle the salt over the cucumber and leave for 30 minutes. Rinse thoroughly in cold water, drain and pat dry with absorbent kitchen paper.

Heat a wok or large frying pan, add the oil and when hot, add the chilli powder, garlic and black beans and stir-fry for 30 seconds. Add the cucumber and stir-fry for 20 seconds.

Pour the stock into the wok and cook for 3–4 minutes, or until the cucumber is very tender. The liquid will have evaporated at this stage. Remove from the heat and stir in the sesame oil. Turn into a warmed serving dish, garnish with chopped parsley and serve immediately.

Try This: FOR AN ALTERNATIVE: 250   FOR FINGER FOOD: 84

Vegetables Braised in Olive Oil & Lemon

SERVES 4

small strip of pared rind and
  juice of ½ lemon
4 tbsp olive oil
1 bay leaf
large sprig of thyme
150 ml/¼ pint water
4 spring onions, trimmed

and finely chopped
175 g/6 oz baby button
  mushrooms
175 g/6 oz broccoli, cut into
  small florets
175 g/6 oz cauliflower, cut
  into small florets

1 medium courgette,
  sliced on the diagonal
2 tbsp freshly
  snipped chives
salt and freshly ground
  black pepper
lemon zest, to garnish

Put the pared lemon rind and juice into a large saucepan. Add the olive oil, bay leaf, thyme and the water. Bring to the boil. Add the spring onions and mushrooms. Top with the broccoli and cauliflower, trying to add them so that the stalks are submerged in the water and the tops are just above it. Cover and simmer for 3 minutes.

Scatter the courgettes on top, so that they are steamed rather than boiled. Cook, covered, for a further 3–4 minutes, until all the vegetables are tender. Using a slotted spoon, transfer the vegetables from the liquid into a warmed serving dish. Increase the heat and boil rapidly for 3–4 minutes, or until the liquid is reduced to about 8 tablespoons. Remove the lemon rind, bay leaf and thyme sprig and discard.

Stir the chives into the reduced liquid, season to taste with salt and pepper and pour over the vegetables. Sprinkle with lemon zest and serve immediately.

Try This: FOR AN ALTERNATIVE: 276   FOR FINGER FOOD: 76

Fettucini with Roasted Beetroot & Rocket

SERVES 4

350 g/12 oz raw baby
   beetroot, unpeeled
1 garlic clove, peeled and
   crushed
½ tsp finely grated

orange rind
1 tbsp orange juice
1 tsp lemon juice
2 tbsp walnut oil
salt and freshly ground

black pepper
350 g/12 oz dried fettucini
75 g/3 oz rocket leaves
125 g/4 oz Dolcelatte cheese,
   cut into small cubes

Preheat oven to 150°C/300°F/Gas Mark 2, 10 minutes before cooking. Wrap the beetroot individually in tinfoil and bake for 1–1½ hours, or until tender. (Test by opening one of the parcels and scraping the skin away from the stem end – it should come off very easily.)

Leave the beetroot until cool enough to handle, then peel and cut each beetroot into 6–8 wedges, depending on the size. Mix the garlic, orange rind and juice, lemon juice, walnut oil and salt and pepper together, then drizzle over the beetroot and toss to coat well.

Meanwhile, bring a large saucepan of lightly salted water to the boil. Cook the pasta for 10 minutes, or until 'al dente'.

Drain the pasta thoroughly, then add the warm beetroot, rocket leaves and Dolcelatte cheese. Quickly and gently toss together, then divide between serving bowls and serve immediately before the rocket wilts.

Try This: FOR AN ALTERNATIVE: 282   FOR FINGER FOOD: 84

Rice–filled Peppers

SERVES 4

8 ripe tomatoes
2 tbsp olive oil
1 onion, peeled and
    chopped
1 garlic clove, peeled and
    crushed
½ tsp dark

muscovado sugar
125 g/4 oz cooked
    long-grain rice
50 g/2 oz pine nuts, toasted
1 tbsp freshly
    chopped oregano
salt and freshly ground

black pepper
2 large red peppers
2 large yellow peppers

To serve:
mixed salad
crusty bread

Preheat oven to 200°C/400°F/Gas Mark 6. Put the tomatoes in a small bowl and pour over boiling water to cover. Leave for 1 minute, then drain. Plunge the tomatoes into cold water to cool, then peel off the skins. Quarter, remove the seeds and chop.

Heat the olive oil in a frying pan, and cook the onion gently for 10 minutes, until softened. Add the garlic, chopped tomatoes and sugar. Gently cook the tomato mixture for 10 minutes until thickened. Remove from the heat and stir the rice, pine nuts and oregano into the sauce. Season to taste with salt and pepper.

Halve the peppers lengthways, cutting through and leaving the stem on. Remove the seeds and cores, then put the peppers in a lightly oiled roasting tin, cut-side down and cook in the preheated oven for about 10 minutes.

Turn the peppers so they are cut-side up. Spoon in the filling, then cover with tinfoil. Return to the oven for 15 minutes, or until the peppers are very tender, removing the tinfoil for the last 5 minutes to allow the tops to brown a little.

Serve 1 red pepper half and 1 yellow pepper half per person with a mixed salad and plenty of warmed, crusty bread.

Try This: FOR AN ALTERNATIVE: 210   FOR FINGER FOOD: 66

Venetian–style Vegetables & Beans

SERVES 4

250 g/9 oz dried pinto beans
3 sprigs of fresh parsley
1 sprig of fresh rosemary
2 tbsp olive oil
200 g can chopped tomatoes
2 shallots, peeled

For the vegetable mixture:
1 large red onion, peeled
1 large white onion, peeled
1 medium carrot, peeled
2 sticks celery, trimmed
3 tbsp olive oil

3 bay leaves
1 tsp caster sugar
3 tbsp red wine vinegar
salt and freshly ground
black pepper

Put the beans in a bowl, cover with plenty of cold water and leave to soak for at least 8 hours, or overnight.

Drain and rinse the beans. Put in a large saucepan with 1.1 litres/2 pints cold water. Tie the parsley and rosemary in muslin and add to the beans with the olive oil. Boil rapidly for 10 minutes, then lower the heat and simmer for 20 minutes with the saucepan half-covered. Stir in the tomatoes and shallots and simmer for a further 10–15 minutes, or until the beans are cooked.

Meanwhile, slice the red and white onion into rings and then finely dice the carrot and celery. Heat the olive oil in a saucepan and cook the onions over a very low heat for about 10 minutes. Add the carrot, celery and bay leaves to the saucepan and cook for a further 10 minutes, stirring frequently, until the vegetables are tender. Sprinkle with sugar, stir and cook for 1 minute.

Stir in the vinegar. Cook for 1 minute, then remove the saucepan from the heat. Drain the beans through a fine sieve, discarding all the herbs, then add the beans to the onion mixture and season well with salt and pepper. Mix gently, then tip the beans into a large serving bowl. Leave to cool, then serve at room temperature.

 Try This: FOR AN ALTERNATIVE: 256   FOR FINGER FOOD: 70

Pasta Primavera

SERVES 4

150 g/5 oz French beans
150 g/5 oz sugar snap peas
40 g/1½ oz butter
1 tsp olive oil
225 g/8 oz baby carrots,
    scrubbed
2 courgettes, trimmed

and thinly sliced
175 g/6 oz baby leeks,
    trimmed and cut into 2.5
    cm/1 inch lengths
200 ml/7 fl oz double cream
1 tsp finely grated lemon rind
350 g/12 oz dried tagliatelle

25 g/1 oz Parmesan
    cheese, grated
1 tbsp freshly snipped chives
1 tbsp freshly chopped dill
salt and freshly ground
    black pepper
sprigs of fresh dill, to garnish

Trim and halve the French beans. Bring a large saucepan of lightly salted water to the boil and cook the beans for 4–5 minutes, adding the sugar snap peas after 2 minutes, so that both are tender at the same time. Drain the beans and sugar snap peas and briefly rinse under cold running water.

Heat the butter and oil in a large non-stick frying pan. Add the baby carrots and cook for 2 minutes, then stir in the courgettes and leeks and cook for 10 minutes, stirring, until the vegetables are almost tender. Stir the cream and lemon rind into the vegetables and bubble over a gentle heat until the sauce is slightly reduced and the vegetables are cooked. Meanwhile, bring a large saucepan of lightly salted water to the boil and cook the tagliatelle for 10 minutes, or until 'al dente'.

Add the beans, sugar snaps, Parmesan cheese and herbs to the sauce. Stir for 30 seconds, or until the cheese has melted and the vegetables are hot.

Drain the tagliatelle, add the vegetables and sauce, then toss gently to mix and season to taste with salt and pepper. Spoon into a warmed serving bowl and garnish with a few sprigs of dill and serve immediately.

Try This: FOR AN ALTERNATIVE: 268   FOR FINGER FOOD: 70

Venetian Herb Orzo

SERVES 4–6

200 g/7 oz baby spinach leaves 150 g/5 oz rocket leaves 50 g/2 oz flat-leaf parsley	6 spring onions, trimmed few leaves of fresh mint 3 tbsp extra virgin olive oil, plus more if required	450 g/11 oz orzo salt and freshly ground black pepper

Rinse the spinach leaves in several changes of cold water and reserve. Finely chop the rocket leaves with the parsley and mint. Thinly slice the green of the spring onions.

Bring a large saucepan of water to the boil, add the spinach leaves, herbs and spring onions and cook for about 10 seconds. Remove and rinse under cold running water. Drain well and, using your hands, squeeze out all the excess moisture.

Place the spinach, herbs and spring onions in a food processor. Blend for 1 minute then, with the motor running, gradually pour in the olive oil until the sauce is well blended.

Meanwhile, bring a large pan of lightly salted water to a rolling boil. Add the pasta and cook according to the packet instructions, or until 'al dente'. Drain thoroughly and place in a large warmed bowl.

Add the spinach sauce to the orzo and stir lightly until the orzo is well coated. Stir in an extra tablespoon of olive oil if the mixture seems too thick. Season well with salt and pepper. Serve immediately on warmed plates or allow to cool to room temperature.

Try This: FOR AN ALTERNATIVE: 252   FOR FINGER FOOD: 84

Fusilli with Courgettes & Sun-dried Tomatoes

SERVES 6

5 tbsp olive oil
1 large onion, peeled and
  thinly sliced
2 garlic cloves, peeled and
  finely chopped
700 g/1½ lb courgettes,
  trimmed and sliced

400 g can chopped
  plum tomatoes
12 sun-dried tomatoes,
  cut into thin strips
salt and freshly ground
  black pepper
450 g/1 lb fusilli

25 g/1 oz butter, diced
2 tbsp freshly chopped basil
  or flat-leaf parsley
grated Parmesan or
  pecorino cheese,
  for serving

Heat 2 tablespoons of the olive oil in a large frying pan, add the onion and cook for 5-7 minutes, or until softened. Add the chopped garlic and courgette slices and cook for a further 5 minutes, stirring occasionally.

Stir the chopped tomatoes and the sun-dried tomatoes into the frying pan and season to taste with salt and pepper. Cook until the courgettes are just tender and the sauce is slightly thickened.

Bring a large pan of lightly salted water to a rolling boil. Add the fusilli and cook according to the packet instructions, or until 'al dente'.

Drain the fusilli thoroughly and return to the pan. Add the butter and remaining oil and toss to coat. Stir the chopped basil or parsley into the courgette mixture and pour over the fusilli. Toss and tip into a warmed serving dish. Serve with grated Parmesan or pecorino cheese.

Try This: FOR AN ALTERNATIVE: 284 FOR FINGER FOOD: 78

Linguine with Walnut Pesto

SERVES 4

125 g/4 oz walnut halves
1–2 garlic cloves, peeled and
   coarsely chopped
40 g/1 ½ oz dried
   breadcrumbs
3 tbsp extra virgin olive oil

1 tbsp walnut oil
3–4 tbsp freshly
   chopped parsley
50 g/2 oz butter, softened
2 tbsp double cream
25 g/1 oz Parmesan cheese,

grated, plus extra
   to serve
salt and freshly ground
   black pepper
450 g/1 lb linguine

Bring a saucepan of water to the boil. Add the walnut halves and simmer for about 1 minute. Drain and turn on to a clean tea towel. Using the towel, rub the nuts gently to loosen the skins, turn into a coarse sieve or colander and shake to separate the skins. Discard the skins and coarsely chop the nuts.

With the the food processor motor running, drop in the garlic cloves and chop finely. Remove the lid, then add the walnuts, breadcrumbs, olive and walnut oils and the parsley. Blend to a paste with a crumbly texture.

Scrape the nut mixture into a bowl, add the softened butter and, using a wooden spoon, cream them together. Gradually beat in the cream and the Parmesan cheese. Season the walnut pesto to taste with salt and pepper.

Bring a large pan of lightly salted water to a rolling boil. Add the linguine and cook according to the packet instructions, or until 'al dente'.

Drain the linguine thoroughly, reserving 1–2 tablespoons of the cooking water. Return the linguine and reserved water to the pan. Add the walnut pesto, 1 tablespoon at a time, tossing and stirring until well coated. Tip into a warmed serving dish or spoon on to individual plates. Serve immediately with the extra grated Parmesan cheese.

Try This: FOR AN ALTERNATIVE: 280   FOR FINGER FOOD: 60

Pumpkin–filled Pasta with Butter & Sage

SERVES 6–8

1 quantity fresh pasta dough
  (*see* page 126)
125 g/4 oz butter
2 tbsp freshly shredded
  sage leaves
50 g/2 oz freshly grated
  Parmesan cheese,
  to serve

For the filling:
250 g/9 oz freshly cooked
  pumpkin or sweet potato
  flesh, mashed and cooled
75–125 g/3–4 oz dried
  breadcrumbs
125 g/4 oz freshly grated
  Parmesan cheese

1 medium egg yolk
½ tsp soft brown sugar
2 tbsp freshly
  chopped parsley
freshly grated nutmeg
salt and freshly ground
  black pepper

Mix together the ingredients for the filling in a bowl, seasoning to taste with freshly grated nutmeg, salt and pepper. If the mixture seems too wet, add a few more breadcrumbs to bind.

Cut the pasta dough into quarters. Work with one quarter at a time, covering the remaining quarters with a damp tea towel. Roll out a quarter very thinly into a strip 10 cm/4 inches wide. Drop spoonfuls of the filling along the strip 6.5 cm/2½ inches apart, in 2 rows about 5 cm/2 inches apart. Moisten the outside edges and the spaces between the filling with water.

Roll out another strip of pasta and lay it over the filled strip. Press down gently along both edges and between the filled sections. Using a fluted pastry wheel, cut along both long sides, down the centre and between the fillings to form cushions. Transfer the cushions to a lightly floured baking sheet. Continue making cushions and allow to dry for 30 minutes.

Bring a large saucepan of slightly salted water to the boil. Add the pasta cushions and return to the boil. Cook, stirring frequently, for 4–5 minutes, or until 'al dente'. Drain carefully. Heat the butter in a pan, stir in the shredded sage leaves and cook for 30 seconds. Add the pasta cushions, stir gently then spoon into serving bowls. Sprinkle with the grated Parmesan cheese and serve immediately.

Try This: FOR AN ALTERNATIVE: 270   FOR FINGER FOOD: 26

Singapore Noodles

SERVES 4

225 g/8 oz thin round
   egg noodles
3 tbsp groundnut or
   vegetable oil
125 g/4 oz field mushrooms,
   wiped and thinly sliced
2.5 cm/1 inch piece root
   ginger, peeled and
   finely chopped
1 red chilli, deseeded and
   thinly sliced

1 red pepper, deseeded
   and thinly sliced
2 garlic cloves, peeled
   and crushed
1 medium courgette, cut in
   half lengthwise and
   diagonally sliced
4–6 spring onions, trimmed
   and thinly sliced
50 g/2 oz frozen garden
   peas, thawed

1 tbsp curry paste
2 tbsp tomato ketchup
salt or soy sauce
125 g/4 oz beansprouts,
   rinsed and drained

To garnish:
sesame seeds
fresh coriander leaves

Bring a large pan of lightly salted water to a rolling boil. Add the noodles and cook according to the packet instructions, or until 'al dente'. Drain thoroughly and toss with 1 tablespoon of the oil.

Heat the remaining oil in a wok or large frying pan over high heat. Add the mushrooms, ginger, chilli and red pepper and stir-fry for 2 minutes. Add the garlic, courgettes, spring onions and garden peas and stir lightly.

Push the vegetables to one side and add the curry paste, tomato ketchup and about 125 ml/4 fl oz hot water. Season to taste with salt or a few drops of soy sauce and allow to boil vigorously, stirring, until the paste is smooth.

Stir the reserved egg noodles and the beansprouts into the vegetable mixture and stir-fry until coated with the paste and thoroughly heated through. Season with more soy sauce if necessary, then turn into a large warmed serving bowl or spoon on to individual plates. Garnish with sesame seeds and coriander leaves. Serve immediately.

Try This: FOR AN ALTERNATIVE: 252   FOR FINGER FOOD: 68

Tortellini & Summer Vegetable Salad

SERVES 6

350 g/12 oz mixed green and plain cheese-filled fresh tortellini
150 ml/¼ pint extra virgin olive oil
225 g/8 oz fine green beans, trimmed
175 g/6 oz broccoli florets
1 yellow or red pepper, deseeded and thinly sliced
1 red onion, peeled and sliced
175 g jar marinated artichoke hearts, drained and halved
2 tbsp capers
75 g/3 oz dry-cured pitted black olives
3 tbsp raspberry or balsamic vinegar
1 tbsp Dijon mustard
1 tsp soft brown sugar
salt and freshly ground black pepper
2 tbsp freshly chopped basil or flat-leaf parsley
2 quartered hard-boiled eggs, to garnish

Bring a large pan of lightly salted water to a rolling boil. Add the tortellini and cook according to the packet instructions, or until 'al dente'. Using a large slotted spoon, transfer the tortellini to a colander to drain. Rinse under cold running water and drain again. Transfer to a large bowl and toss with 2 tablespoons of the olive oil.

Return the pasta water to the boil and drop in the green beans and broccoli florets; blanch them for 2 minutes, or until just beginning to soften. Drain, rinse under cold running water and drain again thoroughly. Add the vegetables to the reserved tortellini.

Add the pepper, onion, artichoke hearts, capers and olives to the bowl; stir lightly.

Whisk together the vinegar, mustard and brown sugar in a bowl and season to taste with salt and pepper. Slowly whisk in the remaining olive oil to form a thick, creamy dressing. Pour over the tortellini and vegetables, add the chopped basil or parsley and stir until lightly coated. Transfer to a shallow serving dish or salad bowl. Garnish with the hard-boiled egg quarters and serve.

Try This: FOR AN ALTERNATIVE: 286   FOR FINGER FOOD: 74

Bulghur Wheat Salad
with Minty Lemon Dressing

SERVES 4

125 g/4 oz bulghur wheat
10 cm /4 inch piece
   cucumber
2 shallots, peeled
125 g/4 oz baby sweetcorn
3 ripe but firm tomatoes

For the dressing:
grated rind of 1 lemon
3 tbsp lemon juice
3 tbsp freshly chopped mint
2 tbsp freshly chopped
   parsley

1–2 tsp clear honey
2 tbsp sunflower oil
salt and freshly ground
   black pepper

Place the bulghur wheat in a saucepan and cover with boiling water. Simmer for about 10 minutes, then drain thoroughly and turn into a serving bowl.

Cut the cucumber into small dice, chop the shallots finely and reserve. Steam the sweetcorn over a pan of boiling water for 10 minutes or until tender. Drain and slice into thick chunks.

Cut a cross on the top of each tomato and place in boiling water until their skins start to peel away. Remove the skins and the seeds and cut the tomatoes into small dice.

Make the dressing by briskly whisking all the ingredients in a small bowl until mixed well.

When the bulghur wheat has cooled a little, add all the prepared vegetables and stir in the dressing. Season to taste with salt and pepper and serve.

Try This: FOR AN ALTERNATIVE: 250   FOR FINGER FOOD: 84

Stuffed Onions with Pine Nuts

SERVES 4

4 medium onions, peeled
2 garlic cloves, peeled
    and crushed
2 tbsp fresh
    brown breadcrumbs
4 tbsp white breadcrumbs

25 g/1 oz sultanas
25 g/1 oz pine nuts
50 g/2 oz low-fat hard
    cheese such as
    Edam, grated
2 tbsp freshly

chopped parsley
salt and freshly ground
    black pepper
1 medium egg, beaten
salad leaves,
    to serve

Preheat the oven to 200°C/400°F/Gas Mark 6. Bring a pan of water to the boil, add the onions and cook gently for about 15 minutes. Drain well. Allow the onions to cool, then slice each one in half horizontally.

Scoop out most of the onion flesh but leave a reasonably firm shell.

Chop up 4 tablespoons of the onion flesh and place in a bowl with the crushed garlic, brown breadcrumbs, 2 tablespoons of the white breadcrumbs, sultanas, pine nuts, grated cheese and parsley. Mix the breadcrumb mixture together thoroughly. Season to taste with salt and pepper. Bind together with as much of the beaten egg as necessary to make a firm filling.

Pile the mixture back into the onion shells and top with the remaining breadcrumbs. Place on a oiled baking tray and cook in the preheated oven for 20–30 minutes or until golden brown. Serve immediately with the salad leaves.

Try This: FOR AN ALTERNATIVE: 208   FOR FINGER FOOD: 84

Beetroot & Potato Medley

SERVES 4

350 g/12 oz raw
   baby beetroot
½ tsp sunflower oil
225 g/8 oz new potatoes
½ cucumber, peeled

3 tbsp white wine vinegar
150 ml/5 fl oz natural
   low-fat yogurt
salt and freshly ground
   black pepper

fresh salad leaves
1 tbsp freshly snipped
   chives, to garnish

Preheat the oven to 180°C/350°F/Gas Mark 4. Scrub the beetroot thoroughly and place on a baking tray. Brush the beetroot with a little oil and cook for 1½ hours or until a skewer is easily insertable into the beetroot. Allow to cool a little, then remove the skins.

Cook the potatoes in boiling water for about 10 minutes. Rinse in cold water and drain. Reserve the potatoes until cool. Dice evenly.

Cut the cucumber into cubes and place in a mixing bowl. Chop the beetroot into small cubes and add to the bowl with the reserved potatoes. Gently mix the vegetables together.

Mix together the vinegar and yogurt and season to taste with a little salt and pepper. Pour over the vegetables and combine gently. Arrange on a bed of salad leaves garnished with the snipped chives and serve.

Try This: FOR AN ALTERNATIVE: 258   FOR FINGER FOOD: 82

Light Ratatouille

SERVES 4

1 red pepper
2 courgettes, trimmed
1 small aubergine, trimmed
1 onion, peeled

2 ripe tomatoes
50 g/2 oz button
   mushrooms, wiped
   and halved or quartered

200 ml/7 fl oz tomato juice
1 tbsp freshly chopped basil
salt and freshly ground
   black pepper

Deseed the peppers, remove the membrane with a small sharp knife and cut into small dice. Thickly slice the courgettes and cut the aubergine into small dice. Slice the onion into rings. Place the tomatoes in boiling water until their skins begin to peel away. Remove the skins from the tomatoes, cut into quarters and remove the seeds.

Place all the vegetables in a saucepan with the tomato juice and basil. Season to taste with salt and pepper. Bring to the boil, cover and simmer for 15 minutes or until the vegetables are tender. Remove the vegetables with a slotted spoon and arrange in a serving dish.

Bring the liquid in the pan to the boil and boil for 20 seconds until it is slightly thickened. Season the sauce to taste with salt and pepper. Pass the sauce through a sieve to remove some of the seeds and pour over the vegetables. Serve the ratatouille hot or cold.

Try This: FOR AN ALTERNATIVE: 268   FOR FINGER FOOD: 80

Indonesian Salad with Peanut Dressing

SERVES 4

225 g/8 oz new potatoes, scrubbed
1 large carrot, peeled and cut into matchsticks
125 g/4 oz French beans, trimmed
225 g/8 oz tiny cauliflower florets
125 g/4 oz cucumber, cut into matchsticks
75 g/3 oz fresh bean sprouts
3 medium eggs, hard-boiled and quartered

For the peanut dressing:
2 tbsp sesame oil
1 garlic clove, peeled and crushed
1 red chilli, deseeded and finely chopped
150 g/5 oz crunchy peanut butter
6 tbsp hot vegetable stock
2 tsp soft light brown sugar
2 tsp dark soy sauce
1 tbsp lime juice

Cook the potatoes in a saucepan of boiling salted water for 15–20 minutes until tender. Remove with a slotted spoon and thickly slice into a large bowl. Keep the saucepan of water boiling.

Add the carrot, French beans and cauliflower to the water, return to the boil and cook for 2 minutes, or until just tender. Drain and refresh under cold running water, then drain well. Add to the potatoes with the cucumber and bean sprouts.

To make the dressing, gently heat the sesame oil in a small saucepan. Add the garlic and chilli and cook for a few seconds, then remove from the heat. Stir in the peanut butter. Stir in the stock, a little at a time. Add the remaining ingredients and mix together to make a thick, creamy dressing.

Divide the vegetables between 4 plates and arrange the eggs on top. Drizzle the dressing over the salad and serve immediately.

Try This: FOR AN ALTERNATIVE: 246   FOR FINGER FOOD: 66

Sweet Treats

Fruit Salad

SERVES 4

125 g/4 oz caster sugar
3 oranges
700 g/1½ lb lychees,
   peeled and stoned
1 small mango
1 small pineapple

1 papaya
4 pieces stem ginger in syrup
4 tbsp stem ginger syrup
125 g/4 oz Cape
   gooseberries
125 g/4 oz strawberries,

hulled (leaves removed)
½ tsp almond essence

To decorate:
lime zest
mint leaves

Place the sugar and 300 ml/½ pint of water in a small pan and heat, gently stirring until the sugar has dissolved. Bring to the boil and simmer for 2 minutes. Once a syrup has formed, remove from the heat and allow to cool.

Using a sharp knife, cut away the skin from the oranges, then slice thickly. Cut each slice in half and place in a serving dish with the syrup and lychees.

Cut the mango lengthways along each side of the stone. To remove the flesh from the skin, score each half lengthways and widthways, then cut away the flesh from skin to make bite-size pieces. Alternatively, peel the mango, then cut into thick slices around each side of the stone before cutting into bite-size pieces. Discard the stone and add the bite-sized pieces to the syrup.

Using a sharp knife again, carefully cut away the skin from the pineapple. Remove the central core using the knife or an apple corer, then cut the pineapple into segments and add to the syrup.

Peel the papaya, then cut in half and remove the seeds. Cut the flesh into chunks, slice the ginger into matchsticks and add with the ginger syrup to the fruit in the syrup. Prepare the Cape gooseberries, by removing the thin, papery skins and rinsing lightly. Halve the strawberries, add to the fruit with the almond essence and chill for 30 minutes. Scatter with mint leaves and lime zest to decorate and serve.

 Try This: FOR AN ALTERNATIVE: 292   FOR A SAVOURY BITE: 66

Crème Brûlée with Sugared Raspberries

SERVES 6

600 ml/1 pint fresh whipping cream
4 medium egg yolks

75 g/3 oz caster sugar
½ tsp vanilla essence
25 g/1 oz demerara sugar

175 g/6 oz fresh raspberries

Preheat the oven to 150°C/300°F/Gas Mark 2. Pour the cream into a bowl and place over a saucepan of gently simmering water. Heat gently but do not allow to boil.

Meanwhile, whisk together the egg yolks, 50 g/2 oz of the caster sugar and the vanilla essence. When the cream is warm, pour it over the egg mixture briskly whisking until it is mixed completely.

Pour into 6 individual ramekin dishes and place in a roasting tin. Fill the tin with sufficient water to come halfway up the sides of the dishes. Bake in the preheated oven for about 1 hour, or until the puddings are set. (To test if set, carefully insert a round bladed knife into the centre, if the knife comes out clean they are set.)

Remove the puddings from the roasting tin and allow to cool. Chill in the refrigerator, preferably overnight.

Sprinkle the sugar over the top of each dish and place the puddings under a preheated hot grill. When the sugar has caramelised and turned deep brown, remove from the heat and cool. Chill the puddings in the refrigerator for 2–3 hours before serving.

Toss the raspberries in the remaining caster sugar and sprinkle over the top of each dish. Serve with a little extra cream if liked.

Try This: FOR AN ALTERNATIVE: 290   FOR A SAVOURY BITE: 74

Chocolate Mousse

SERVES 6

175 g/6 oz milk or plain
chocolate orange
535 g carton half-fat
ready-made custard

450 ml/¾ pint half-fat
double cream
12 Cape gooseberries,
to decorate

sweet, reduced-fat biscuits,
to serve

Break the chocolate into segments and place in a bowl set over a saucepan of simmering water. Leave until melted, stirring occasionally. Remove the bowl in the pan from the heat and allow the melted chocolate to cool slightly.

Place the custard in a bowl and fold the melted chocolate into it using a metal spoon or rubber spatula. Stir well until completely combined.

Pour the cream into a small bowl and whip until the cream forms soft peaks. Using a metal spoon or rubber spatula fold in most of the whipped cream into the chocolate mixture.

Spoon into six tall glasses and carefully top with the remaining cream. Leave the desserts to chill in the refrigerator for at least 1 hour or preferably overnight.

Peel back the skins from the gooseberries to form petal shapes and use to decorate the chocolate desserts. Serve with sweet reduced-fat biscuits.

Try This: FOR AN ALTERNATIVE: 296   FOR A SAVOURY BITE: 80

Spicy White Chocolate Mousse

SERVES 4–6

6 cardamom pods
125 ml/4 fl oz milk
3 bay leaves

200 g/7 oz white chocolate
300 ml/½ pint double cream
3 medium egg whites

1–2 tsp cocoa powder,
sifted, for dusting

Tap the cardamom pods lightly so they split. Remove the seeds, then, using a pestle and mortar, crush lightly. Pour the milk into a small saucepan and add the crushed seeds and the bay leaves. Bring to the boil gently over a medium heat. Remove from the heat, cover and leave in a warm place for at least 30 minutes to infuse.

Break the chocolate into small pieces and place in a heatproof bowl set over a saucepan of gently simmering water. Ensure the water is not touching the base of the bowl. When the chocolate has melted remove the bowl from the heat and stir until smooth.

Whip the cream until it has slightly thickened and holds its shape, but does not form peaks. Reserve. Whisk the egg whites in a clean, grease-free bowl until stiff and standing in soft peaks.

Strain the milk through a sieve into the cooled, melted chocolate and beat until smooth. Spoon the chocolate mixture into the egg whites, then using a large metal spoon, fold gently. Add the whipped cream and fold in gently.

Spoon into a large serving dish or individual small cups. Chill in the refrigerator for 3–4 hours. Just before serving, dust with a little sifted cocoa powder and then serve.

 Try This: FOR AN ALTERNATIVE: 294   FOR A SAVOURY BITE: 66

'Mars' Bar Mousse in Filo Cups

SERVES 6

6 large sheets filo pastry,
  thawed if frozen
40 g/1½ oz unsalted butter,
  melted
1 tbsp caster sugar
3 x 60 g/2½ oz 'Mars' bars,

  coarsely chopped
1½ tbsp milk
300 ml/½ pint double cream
1 large egg white
1 tsp cocoa powder
1 tbsp dark grated chocolate

For the topping:
300 ml/½ pint whipping
  cream
125 g/4 oz white
  chocolate, grated
1 tsp vanilla essence

Preheat the oven to 180°C/ 350°F/Gas Mark 4, 10 minutes before baking. Lightly oil 6 x 150 ml/¼ pint ramekins. Cut the filo pastry into 15 cm/6 inch squares, place 1 square on the work surface, then brush with a little of the melted butter, sprinkle with a little caster sugar. Butter a second square and lay it over the first at an angle, sprinkle with a little more caster sugar and repeat with 2 more pastry squares.

Press the assembled filo pastry into the oiled ramekin, pressing into the base to make a flat bottom and keeping the edges pointing up. Continue making the cups in this way, then place on a baking sheet and bake in the preheated oven for 10–15 minutes or until crisp and golden. Remove and leave to cool before removing the filo cups from the ramekins.

Melt the 'Mars' bars and milk in a saucepan, stirring constantly until melted and smooth. Leave to cool for 10 minutes, stirring occasionally. Whisk the cream until thick and stir a spoonful into the 'Mars' bar mixture, then fold in the remaining cream. Whisk the egg white until stiff and fold into the mixture together with the cocoa powder. Chill in the refrigerator for 2–3 hours.

For the topping, boil 125 ml/4 fl oz of the whipping cream, add the grated white chocolate and vanilla essence and stir until smooth, then strain into a bowl and leave to cool. Whisk the remaining cream until thick, then fold into the white chocolate cream mixture. Spoon the mousse into the filo cups, cover with the cream mixture and sprinkle with grated chocolate. Chill in the refrigerator before serving.

Try This: FOR AN ALTERNATIVE: 294   FOR A SAVOURY BITE: 20

Chocolate Creams

SERVES 4

125 g/4 oz plain
   dark chocolate
1 tbsp brandy
4 medium eggs, separated

200 ml/7 fl oz pint
   double cream
1 tbsp caster sugar
grated rind of 1 orange

2 tbsp Cointreau
25 g/1 oz white chocolate
8 Cape gooseberries
   (Physalis fruit), to decorate

Break the chocolate into small pieces, then place in a heatproof bowl set over a saucepan of gently simmering water. Add the brandy and heat gently, stirring occasionally until the chocolate has melted and is smooth. Remove from the heat and leave to cool slightly, then beat in the egg yolks, 1 at a time, beating well after each addition. Reserve.

Whisk the egg whites until stiff but not dry, then stir 1 tablespoon into the chocolate mixture. Add the remainder and stir in gently. Chill in the refrigerator while preparing the cream.

Whip the cream until just beginning to thicken, then stir in the sugar, orange rind and Cointreau and continue to whisk together until soft peaks form. Spoon the chocolate mousse into the cream mixture and using a metal spoon, fold the 2 mixtures together to create a marbled effect. Alternatively, continue folding the 2 mixtures together until mixed thoroughly. Spoon into 4 individual glass dishes, cover each dessert with clingfilm and chill in the refrigerator for 2 hours.

Using a potato peeler, shave the white chocolate into curls. Uncover the desserts and scatter over the shavings. Peel the husks back from the physalis berries and pinch together for decoration. Top each dessert with 2 berries and chill in the refrigerator until ready to serve.

Try This: FOR AN ALTERNATIVE: 296   FOR A SAVOURY BITE: 82

Chocolate Chip Cookies

MAKES 36 BISCUITS

175 g/6 oz plain flour
pinch of salt
1 tsp baking powder

¼ tsp bicarbonate of soda
75 g/3 oz butter or margarine
50 g/2 oz soft light

brown sugar
3 tbsp golden syrup
125 g/4 oz chocolate chips

Preheat the oven to 190°C/375°F/Gas Mark 5, 10 minutes before baking. Lightly oil a large baking sheet.

In a large bowl, sift together the flour, salt, baking powder and bicarbonate of soda. Cut the butter or margarine into small pieces and add to the flour mixture. Using 2 knives or the fingertips, rub in the butter or margarine until the mixture resembles coarse breadcrumbs. Add the light brown sugar, golden syrup and chocolate chips. Mix together until a smooth dough forms.

Shape the mixture into small balls and arrange on the baking sheet, leaving enough space to allow them to expand. (These cookies do not increase in size by a great deal, but allow a little space for expansion.) Flatten the mixture slightly with the fingertips or the heel of the hand. Bake in the preheated oven for 12–15 minutes, or until golden and cooked through.

Allow to cool slightly, then transfer the biscuits on to a wire rack to cool. Serve when cold or otherwise store in an airtight tin.

Try This: FOR AN ALTERNATIVE: 304   FOR A SAVOURY BITE: 72

Honey & Chocolate Hearts

MAKES ABOUT 20

60 g/2½ oz caster sugar
15 g/½ oz butter
125 g/4 oz thick honey
1 small egg, beaten

pinch of salt
1 tbsp mixed peel or chopped
glacé ginger
¼ tsp ground cinnamon

pinch of ground cloves
225 g/8 oz plain flour, sifted
½ tsp baking powder, sifted
75 g/3 oz milk chocolate

Preheat the oven to 220°C/425°F/Gas Mark 7, 15 minutes before baking. Lightly oil 2 baking sheets. Heat the sugar, butter and honey together in a small saucepan until everything has melted and the mixture is smooth.

Remove from the heat and stir until slightly cooled, then add the beaten egg with the salt and beat well. Stir in the mixed peel or glacé ginger, ground cinnamon, ground cloves, the flour and the baking powder and mix well until a dough is formed. Wrap in clingfilm and chill in the refrigerator for 45 minutes.

Place the chilled dough on a lightly floured surface, roll out to about 5 mm/¼ inch thickness and cut out small heart shapes. Place onto the prepared baking sheets and bake in the preheated oven for 8–10 minutes. Remove from the oven and leave to cool slightly. Using a spatula, transfer to a wire rack until cold.

Melt the chocolate in a heatproof bowl set over a saucepan of simmering water. Alternatively, melt the chocolate in the microwave according to the manufacturer's instructions, until smooth. Dip one half of each biscuit in the melted chocolate. Leave to set before serving.

Try This: FOR AN ALTERNATIVE: 302   FOR A SAVOURY BITE: 28

Light White Chocolate & Walnut Blondies

MAKES 15

75 g/3 oz unsalted butter
200 g/7 oz demerara sugar
2 large eggs, lightly beaten
1 tsp vanilla essence
2 tbsp milk

125 g/4 oz plain flour,
   plus 1 tbsp
1 tsp baking powder
pinch of salt
75 g/3 oz walnuts, roughly

   chopped
125 g/4 oz white
   chocolate drops
1 tbsp icing sugar

Preheat the oven to 190°C/375°F/Gas Mark 5, 10 minutes before baking. Oil and line a 28 x 18 x 2.5 cm/11 x 7 x 1 inch cake tin with nonstick baking parchment. Place the butter and demerara sugar into a heavy-based saucepan and heat gently until the butter has melted and the sugar has started to dissolve. Remove from the heat and leave to cool.

Place the eggs, vanilla essence and milk in a large bowl and beat together. Stir in the butter and sugar mixture, then sift in the 125 g/4oz of flour, the baking powder and salt. Gently stir the mixture twice.

Toss the walnuts and chocolate drops in the remaining 1 tablespoon of flour to coat. Add to the bowl and stir the ingredients together gently.

Spoon the mixture into the prepared tin and bake on the centre shelf of the preheated oven for 35 minutes, or until the top is firm and slightly crusty. Place the tin on a wire rack and leave to cool.

When completely cold, remove the cake from the tin and lightly dust the top with icing sugar. Cut into 15 blondies, using a sharp knife, and serve.

Try This: FOR AN ALTERNATIVE: 314   FOR A SAVOURY BITE: 30

Chocolate Florentines

MAKES 20

125 g/4 oz butter or
    margarine
125 g/4 oz soft light
    brown sugar
1 tbsp double cream
50 g/2 oz blanched almonds,
    roughly chopped

50 g/2 oz hazelnuts,
    roughly chopped
75 g/3 oz sultanas
50 g/2 oz glacé cherries,
    roughly chopped
40 g/1½ oz plain flour
50 g/2 oz plain, dark chocolate,

roughly chopped or broken
50 g/2 oz milk chocolate,
    roughly chopped
    or broken
50 g/2 oz white chocolate,
    roughly chopped or
    broken

Preheat the oven to 180°C/350°F/Gas Mark 4, 10 minutes before baking. Lightly oil a baking sheet.

Melt the butter or margarine with the sugar and double cream in a small saucepan over a very low heat. Do not boil. Remove from the heat and stir in the almonds, hazelnuts, sultanas, cherries and then the flour.

Drop teaspoonfuls of the mixture on to the baking sheet. Transfer to the preheated oven and bake for 10 minutes, until golden.

Leave the biscuits to cool on the baking sheet for about 5 minutes, then carefully transfer to a wire rack to cool.

Melt the plain, milk and white chocolates in separate bowls, either in the microwave following the manufacturers' instructions or in a small bowl, placed over a saucepan of gently simmering water. Spread one-third of the biscuits with the plain chocolate, one-third with the milk chocolate and one-third with the white chocolate.

Mark out wavy lines on the chocolate when almost set with the tines of a fork. Or dip some of the biscuits in chocolate to half coat and serve.

Try This: FOR AN ALTERNATIVE: 304   FOR A SAVOURY BITE: 62

Ginger Snaps

MAKES 40

300 g/11 oz butter or
    margarine, softened
225 g/8 oz soft light
    brown sugar
75 g/3 oz black treacle

1 medium egg
400 g/14 oz plain flour
2 tsp bicarbonate of soda
½ tsp salt
1 tsp ground ginger

1 tsp ground cloves
1 tsp ground cinnamon
50 g/2 oz granulated sugar

Preheat the oven to 190°C/375°F/Gas Mark 5, 10 minutes before baking. Lightly oil a baking sheet.

Cream together the butter or margarine and the sugar until light and fluffy. Warm the treacle in the microwave for 30–40 seconds, then add gradually to the butter mixture with the egg. Beat until combined well.

In a separate bowl, sift the flour, bicarbonate of soda, salt, ground ginger, ground cloves and ground cinnamon. Add to the butter mixture and mix together to form a firm dough.

Chill in the refrigerator for 1 hour. Shape the dough into small balls and roll in the granulated sugar. Place well apart on the oiled baking sheet.

Sprinkle the baking sheet with a little water and transfer to the preheated oven. Bake for 12 minutes, until golden and crisp. Transfer to a wire rack to cool and serve.

Try This: FOR AN ALTERNATIVE: 302   FOR A SAVOURY BITE: 42

Almond Macaroons

MAKES 12

rice paper
125 g/4 oz caster sugar
50 g/2 oz ground almonds

1 tsp ground rice
2–3 drops almond essence
1 medium egg white

8 blanched almonds,
   halved

Preheat the oven to 150°C/300°F/Gas Mark 2, 10 minutes before baking. Line a baking sheet with the rice paper.

Mix the caster sugar, ground almonds, ground rice and almond essence together and reserve.

Whisk the egg white until stiff then gently fold in the caster sugar mixture with a metal spoon or rubber spatula. Mix to form a stiff but not sticky paste. (If the mixture is very sticky, add a little extra ground almonds.)

Place small spoonfuls of the mixture, about the size of an apricot, well apart on the rice paper. Place a half-blanched almond in the centre of each. Place in the preheated oven and bake for 25 minutes, or until just pale golden.

Remove the biscuits from the oven and leave to cool for a few minutes on the baking sheet. Cut or tear the rice paper around the macaroons to release them. Once cold, serve or otherwise store them in an airtight tin.

Try This: FOR AN ALTERNATIVE: 308   FOR A SAVOURY BITE: 60

Lemon Bars

MAKES 24

175 g/6 oz plain flour
125 g/4 oz butter
50 g/2 oz granulated sugar
200 g/7 oz caster sugar
2 tbsp flour

½ tsp baking powder
¼ tsp salt
2 medium eggs,
   lightly beaten
juice and finely grated

rind of 1 lemon
sifted icing sugar,
   to decorate

Preheat the oven to 170°C/325°F/Gas Mark 3, 10 minutes before baking. Lightly oil and line a 20.5 cm/8 inch square cake tin with greaseproof or baking paper.

Rub together the flour and butter until the mixture resembles breadcrumbs. Stir in the granulated sugar and mix. Turn the mixture into the prepared tin and press down firmly. Bake in the preheated oven for 20 minutes, until pale golden.

Meanwhile, in a food processor, mix together the caster sugar, flour, baking powder, salt, eggs, lemon juice and rind until smooth. Pour over the prepared base. Transfer to the preheated oven and bake for a further 20–25 minutes, until nearly set but still a bit wobbly in the centre. Remove from the oven and cool in the tin on a wire rack.

Dust with icing sugar and cut into squares. Serve cold or store in an airtight tin.

Try This: FOR AN ALTERNATIVE: 316   FOR A SAVOURY BITE: 58

Cappuccino Cakes

MAKES 6

125 g/4 oz butter or
    margarine
125 g/4 oz caster sugar
2 medium eggs

1 tbsp strong black coffee
150 g/5 oz self-raising flour
125 g/4 oz mascarpone
    cheese

1 tbsp icing sugar, sifted
1 tsp vanilla essence
sifted cocoa powder,
    to dust

Preheat the oven to 190°C/375°F/Gas Mark 5, 10 minutes before baking. Place 6 large paper muffin cases into a muffin tin or alternatively place on to a baking sheet.

Cream the butter or margarine and sugar together until light and fluffy. Break the eggs into a small bowl and beat lightly with a fork. Using a wooden spoon beat the eggs into the butter and sugar mixture a little at a time, until they are all incorporated.

If the mixture looks curdled beat in a spoonful of the flour to return the mixture to a smooth consistency. Finally beat in the black coffee.

Sift the flour into the mixture, then with a metal spoon or rubber spatula gently fold in the flour.

Place spoonfuls of the mixture into the muffin cases. Bake in the preheated oven for 20–25 minutes, or until risen and springy to the touch. Cool on a wire rack.

In a small bowl beat together the mascarpone cheese, icing sugar and vanilla essence.

When the cakes are cold, spoon the vanilla mascarpone on to the top of each one. Dust with cocoa powder and serve. Eat within 24 hours and store in the refrigerator.

Try This: FOR AN ALTERNATIVE: 314   FOR A SAVOURY BITE: 52

Index